DIVERSITY:
NEW APPROACHES TO
ETHNIC MINORITY AGING

E. Percil Stanford
and
Fernando M. Torres-Gil, *Editors*

GENERATIONS AND AGING SERIES

Originally published as the Fall/Winter 1991 issue of GENERATIONS, Journal of the American Society on Aging, Mary Johnson, Editor.

Baywood Publishing Co. ..ny, Inc.
Amityville, New York

Library of Congress Catalog Number: 92-16836
ISBN: 0-89503-102-7

Library of Congress Cataloging-in-Publication Data

Diversity : new approaches to ethnic minority aging / E. Percil
    Stanford and Fernando M. Torres-Gil, editors.
            p.   cm. – – (Generations and aging series)
        "Originally published as the Fall/Winter 1991 issue of
    Generations, journal of the American Society on Aging."
        Includes bibliographical references.
        ISBN 0-89503-102-7
        1. Minority aged– –United States– –Attitudes.   2. Social work with
    the aged– –United States.   3. Social work with minorities– –United
    States.   I. Stanford, E. Percil.   II. Torres-Gil, Fernando M.
    III. Series.
    HQ1064.U5D59   1992
    305.26– –dc20   92-16836
                                                                                      CIP

Table of Contents

Chapter 1

Diversity and Beyond:
A Commentary

E. Percil Stanford and Fernando M. Torres-Gil

INTRODUCTION

As populations continue to age and individuals live longer, chances of sharing cultural values and normative expectations are apt to increase. With this prospect in mind, it is no longer reasonable to expect that populations will exist in isolated environments. A higher percentage of all persons throughout the world are more likely to find themselves interacting on a global basis. Circumstances may be such that many will permanently change their formal residence. Such change may be interstate, intercontinental, or international. These changes often give people cause to confront personal and cultural biases in unexpected ways, and these biases are not necessarily negative in nature. It is merely that ethnic and cultural underpinnings are a manifestation of one's unique experiences.

During the 1960s, it was popular to voice one's opinions, from a philosophical or practical perspective, regarding ethnicity, race, culture, discrimination, and prejudice. Many had very definite philosophical positions that guided their actions and relations regarding ethnicity and race. Since then, society has continued to evolve with a highly mixed ethnic and racial population. The development of this type of population has made it necessary for all age groups and social classes to reexamine the significance of being able to effectively participate in and contribute to a highly diverse society.

The rapidly burgeoning aging population, which consists of a higher percentage of ethnically and culturally different older people than ever before, is cause for concern but not alarm. With the prospect of approximately 65 million persons—22 percent of the U.S. population—being 65 and older by the year 2030, there is an urgent need to plan for the acceptance, recognition, and utilization of the skills and talents of diverse groups.

That aging population will become increasingly diverse by race, gender, income, ethnicity, immigration, and language. What we now see in the younger population, with its tremendous growth of minority groups, we will see in time in the older population. That diversity raises issues of how we can best respond to different social, cultural, and economic needs; understand and incorporate the effects of race, language, ethnicity, immigration, and historical experiences on the aging process; and in turn make public benefits and programs responsive to that diversity.

Diversity in the older population will require us to distinguish between that which is generic and common to all older persons irrespective of race, language, and ethnicity, on the one hand, and those particular factors that necessitate culturally and linguistically specific responses, on the other. Diversity will challenge us to address potential divisiveness and separation of older groups based on race and ethnicity while we also seek to respond to the common needs of all persons.

The aging network is not alone in facing those challenges. The entire nation is forced to confront them as the U.S. population becomes more diverse, with greater numbers of non-Europeans (African Americans, Hispanics, Asian/Pacific Islanders, Native Americans) and newly arrived immigrant groups from Eastern Europe, the Soviet Union, and the Middle East constituting a larger proportion of the society.

Those challenges will require us to redefine the concept of diversity—from one emphasizing differences and the separation of a population into its isolated parts to one that looks at the strengthening of each group while seeking commonalities that lend themselves to public responses.

There are compelling reasons to go beyond the common definition of diversity. The concept can be used not only to explain variance, differences, and dissimilarities but also to highlight strengths within groups. If we dare focus on the distinctiveness of individuals and groups, numerous positive lessons can be learned.

This new focus is timely because we have been moving away from the old view of our society as a melting pot—in which individuals and cultures were seen as inevitably moving closer together—to a point where there is a push for more tolerance for differences among divergent populations. This shift is accompanied by a degree of uncertainty and lack of understanding regarding when diversity is a strength and when it becomes a liability. We should move toward a notion of diversity that allows for the coexistence of different cultures and ethnic identities while extracting the best from all involved. As this understanding develops, diversity will need to incorporate the notion of acculturation—where the goal is to enable individuals to function successfully in society by eliminating such barriers as racism and nativism (favoring native-born citizens against immigrants) and promoting economic and social opportunities. The concept of acculturation is in contrast to assimilation, whereby one gives up the strengths of group identity.

There are very few, if any, critical areas in society that will escape the effects of diversity and efforts to come to terms with assimilation and acculturation as related to aging. As generations evolve, it will become more evident that diversity will continue to be a leading force in determining the essence of lifestyles of older people as anchors in society.

These ideas and perspectives represent a preliminary examination of some of the evolutionary and future considerations for diversity in aging. This commentary is intended to provide only a point of departure for thinking further about diversity and its significance in the realm of aging. Diversity should be viewed as an enabling concept and not an end unto itself.

Chapter 2

Trends and Forces:
Influence of Immigration, Migration,
and Acculturation on the Fabric
of Aging in America

Donald Gelfand and Barbara W. K. Yee

Predicting trends and forces that will hold into the next century is, in some respects, akin to forecasting from a crystal ball. In gerontology, predictions are difficult because many of the factors that will affect the fabric of aging in America in the coming years are as yet unknown. What all indicators do suggest is a growing diversity in the aging population. As a society we must be prepared to address this likely characteristic of our future.

Increased immigration into the United States is currently having a major impact on the diversity of the American population, just as immigration has shaped the composition of American society throughout our history. Some of the significant changes in immigration flows that have occurred during the past 25 years are attributable to modifications in immigration policy.

RECENT IMMIGRATION POLICY

The first major change was the abandonment in 1965 of the "quota system" that discriminated against individuals from Southern and

Eastern Europe. This system was replaced by one that gave "preference" to close relatives of American citizens, with the result being increased immigration from countries such as Greece, Italy, and Portugal. For the first time since the early 1900s there was also a substantial immigration from Asia.

The Refugee Act of 1980 brought the United States into line with other countries in its definition of a refugee. The application of the criterion "a well-founded fear of persecution" has, however, been political. Cubans, Southeast Asians, and Russian Jews, for example, have not had difficulty obtaining refugee status, while few Central and South Americans have been able to satisfy the Immigration and Naturalization Service about their claims to refugee status. Besides the Cuban "Marielitos" of the 1980s, the largest group of refugees have been the 800,000 Vietnamese who have resettled in the United States, along with a considerable number of Laotians and Cambodians.

None of the immigration reforms successfully dealt with the problems of illegal immigration. After long and bitter debate, the Immigration Reform and Control Act (IRCA) was passed in 1986. Among its most important provisions was a one-year amnesty period during which individuals who had been in the United States since before January 1, 1982, could apply for legalization. In addition, agricultural workers who could prove that they had worked for 90 days between May 1985 and May 1986 were eligible for legalization. Approximately 1.6 million individuals applied for regular legalization and 1.3 million for legalization as Special Agricultural Workers (Baker, 1990). Regular legalization applicants had to prove competency in English within 18 months after the initial legalization approval and apply for permanent residency status one year after this period. The IRCA also required new employees to prove U.S. citizenship or legalized alien status and imposed penalties on employers who hire undocumented workers.

AGING, IMMIGRATION, AND THE FUTURE AGED

Immigration has dramatically increased the representation of some groups in the American population. The percentage of Hispanics in the United States grew from 6.4 in 1980 to 9 in 1990. During the same period the percentage of Asians/Pacific Islanders almost doubled, from 1.5 to 2.9. Overall, more than a third of the population growth in the United States during the 1980s can be attributed to immigration (Vobedja, 1991). As yet, the impact of the increased American diversity on the field of aging either has not been felt or has been overlooked.

High fertility rates have kept the median age among groups such as Hispanics relatively low. Among Southeast Asians and other refugee groups, the proportion of older individuals also tends to be low because of the hardships of migration. Many older persons stay in their homeland if some of their family members remain behind.

Based on fertility rates and immigration patterns among ethnic minority aged, it is possible to project a scenario that will face service providers during the next 30 years. There will be three groups of ethnic minority aged. One group will include native-born blacks, Hispanics, Asians/Pacific Islanders as well as increasing numbers of American Indians. A second group will consist of ethnic minority elderly who immigrated when they were children or young adults. This group includes blacks, Hispanics, and Asians/Pacific Islanders. The third group will be immigrants who have come to this country as older persons.

LIFE-SPAN PERSPECTIVE:
IMPACT OF COHORT AND ACCULTURATION

The life-span perspective enhances our ability to view trends and forces that will impinge upon cohorts into the next century (Barresi, 1987). "Cohort" describes a group of people who share a common factor, such as age. Each age cohort has experienced a set of historical events and trends, including socialization and educational and cultural influences, during the group's lifetime. These life experiences systematically affect the cohort's attitudes, values, beliefs, and behaviors.

Future age cohorts of minority elders will have more diverse characteristics than has been common because the life experiences of members will have been more varied. Age cohorts of minority elders will be less likely to have common immigration histories, socialization patterns, cultural values or behaviors, and educational or socioeconomic backgrounds. Future immigration will include a mixed group of immigrants, particularly if the immigration quotas provide a preference for "skilled" workers as well as for reunification of families. Perhaps the best use of "cohort" for immigrant and ethnic minority elders will be to describe homogeneous groups of immigrants who come to American shores at specific historical times in the future.

Key developmental tasks during the second half of life have not changed dramatically in the United States and will probably remain essentially the same in the near future. For instance, during middle age the major focus is upon reaching a career pinnacle when biological, cognitive, and other skills based upon years of experience coalesce or reach their height. This may mean different things for men and women in our society or for people who come from cultures with differing expectations for people at each stage of the life cycle (Yee, 1989).

Goals for middle age and old age may not be attainable for the older immigrant. When these goals are not reached by late middle age, the responsibility for accomplishing these goals for the family is transferred to the younger generation (Yee, in press). A positive result is the push among Asian immigrant families toward high educational achievement for children. A negative effect is academic burnout when this educational push puts too much stress and responsibility on the younger generation to achieve for the sake of the family.

An immigrant elderly person who came to the United States during his young adult years will probably be quite different from another elder who immigrated recently. The expectations, adaptational requirements, and skills available to cope with old age in America will be quite different for these groups of immigrant elders. The process of acculturation during the intervening years, from immigration to old age, will determine the characteristics of a minority elder. For instance, the Asian and Pacific Islander population will include elderly people who arrived yesterday and also those whose ancestors came to America to work the plantations in Hawaii during the late 1800s.

Acculturation to all American norms may not necessarily be ideal; in fact, in some situations, it may be harmful. For instance, there is some indication that adoption of such habits as high-fat and low-fiber diets may create health problems for immigrants acculturating to American ways (Lipson and Kato-Palmer, 1988; Tong, 1991; Yano et al., 1985). By adopting these harmful habits, Asian and Hispanic Americans and American Indians may become more susceptible to diabetes and heart disease (Morioka-Douglas, 1990; Yee, 1990a). Moreover, psychological and cultural factors such as culturally based stress responses, nutritional patterns, or types of physical activity may account for some of the differences in rates of many preventable diseases (Hahn et al., 1990; Yee, 1990b).

The individual's adherence to traditional cultural norms and acculturation to a new society's cultural norms form an important research agenda. The topics for research include not only those typically viewed as cultural, such as language and family patterns, but also consideration of the relative effects of socioeconomic status versus cultural components of poverty.

MEETING THE NEEDS

It is doubtful that the 1990s and beyond will be a period of expansion for many aging services. The most reasonable approach to meeting the needs of immigrant aged is the maintenance of existing service delivery models with an eye toward revisions that will enhance their effectiveness with this unique—and diverse—population.

Programs that provide orientation to American lifestyle and cultural differences must be segregated for age and gender. English language classes should be given for children, young adults, and middle-aged and elderly students. Mixed-age orientation classes have often turned immigrant and refugee elders away from learning English and learning about their new country. Their younger counterparts in the same classes seem more adept at acquiring these skills. Elders may drop out of these classes because their role-reversed positions in the classroom often seem to them quite shameful and demeaning.

Professionals who work in aging services must be trained to work with diverse ethnic minorities, social classes, and educational levels. The key is sensitivity to diversity and open mindedness about philosophies of life that may be different from one's own value orientations. This training produces professionals who are more tolerant of people from different backgrounds, more accepting of those differences, and able to translate understanding of cultural differences into effective practices with multicultural clients. Basic language skills, such as knowledge of key words and conversational phrases in the languages of clients most likely to be served, should be a component of these training programs. In addition, increased training of health and mental health workers who themselves are from the immigrant and minority groups helps address their special needs.

Mental Health

Life-span developmental goals, cultural identity, and acculturation are of great significance for the immigrant elderly population, but when faced with immediate demands of adjusting to a new society and learning a new language, the immigrant may place these issues in abeyance. As time passes and the demands of daily life in the United States become more routine, the psychological issues of identity may reappear. Dealing with the issues of loss, grief, and depression should be addressed during each phase of adaptation to a new culture.

These issues may be more difficult to resolve for older immigrants who are homebound because they are providing childcare, cooking, and housekeeping so that their adult children can work outside the home (Gelfand, 1988; Yee, 1989; Yee, in press). Being homebound may also be a consequence of the older immigrant's insecurity about using public transportation, a lack of facility in English, inability to find a job, and discomfort about interactions with older people from other ethnic backgrounds.

Mental health interventions for the immigrant aged cannot rely on standard therapeutic interventions. Counseling with the older person about strategies for coping with the new society is important, but not sufficient. Instead, efforts are needed to allow the older immigrants to participate in activities with other members of their own culture. Within these groups individuals may be able to maintain their self-identity and self-esteem based on traditional ethnic values. They may discover new outlets for their abilities.

The provision of programs for immigrant elders places extensive demands on space as well as staff. Few cities or counties have adequate resources to support separate senior centers for Cambodian or Vietnamese elders as well as for elders from El Salvador or Mexico. Larger centers may, however, be able to allot some space within a center at specific times for various ethnic groups.

Even if programs and services are able to make provision for the disparate groups within their community, barriers—such as transportation problems and dependence of immigrant families on their elders for childcare—often prevent immigrant aged from attending programs and receiving services. Perhaps services for different generations of immigrant families could be housed together so that childcare could be provided while elders used aging services during part of the day. The status quo, which all too often has the immigrant elder isolated and homebound as a childcare provider or watching videotapes in the mother tongue, does not begin to meet the mental health needs of this population.

An integration of social, health, and mental health services under one roof in ethnically dense neighborhoods has also been suggested. In areas with large number of ethnic elders, "satellite clinics" could be opened. These multipurpose centers could lower barriers to the use of mental health services while consolidating translators and cultural specialists able to help elders with a variety of needed services.

For these programs to be effective, more efforts at outreach to ethnic and immigrant communities must be made. Mental health crisis intervention and outreach teams are possible in large cities. Similar to ambulance emergency units, these teams would have members who specialize in different languages and cross-cultural psychology. One team could provide service to all areas of the city.

Health

Health needs of the immigrant aged vary by age and ethnic group. There are probably more individuals in their late 60s and 70s among the population entering the United States with immigrant visas than among refugees and illegal aliens, who are typically younger. These differences are attributable to the hardships that face refugees fleeing from persecution and the desire of illegal aliens to obtain work. Among both refugees and illegal aliens, an older person may represent a handicap for successful passage out of their native country and into the United States. Once arrived in the United States, both of these groups may send for their parents, but the majority of these parents are between the ages of 55 and 65 (Gelfand, 1989).

At this age, many of the parents' health problems are due to poor living conditions in the old country and irregular healthcare. Among immigrants in their 70s a larger proportion of individuals will have chronic conditions associated with aging. Meeting the needs of both groups requires health practitioners who are sensitive to major cultural attitudes toward healthcare.

For example, tendencies to express mental health problems in terms of bodily symptoms—somatization—is common among some Hispanic and Asian groups. Integration of health and mental health services would facilitate treatment goals for these two groups. Cultural beliefs concerning etiology and appropriate treatments for illness must be understood by healthcare professionals who treat immigrant elders. Strong culturally defined norms about "hot" and "cold" forces as explanations for illness and disease, for example, are common among Southeast Asians and differ markedly from Western concepts. There are also variations among ethnic groups in allowable eye contact, standards of modesty, and permissible discussion of sexual practices. Understanding these differences is a prerequisite for effective communication between patient and healthcare provider. Communication may also be hampered by the inability of the immigrant older person to describe health problems in English. The healthcare provider needs fluency in the immigrant's mother tongue or an interpreter to allow clear communication about symptoms and treatment.

Even if the provider is able to effectively define the nature of the health problem, he or she needs to be aware of the older immigrants' acceptance of various types of treatment. Women working with some older immigrant men, for example, may find strong resistance to their participation as primary healthcare providers.

The barriers imposed by cultural differences between first-generation immigrant aged and healthcare providers can be major, but provision of adequate healthcare for illegal immigrant aged is even more difficult because of their immigration status. As illegal immigrants, this population is ineligible for any federally funded programs like Medicaid. Many states and localities do not ask an individual's immigration status before providing healthcare, but many illegals are afraid of services that require any documentation or signatures.

Since the majority of illegal aliens do not possess health insurance, they are also forced to use public clinics, emergency rooms, or clinics run by groups such as the Catholic church. Despite the valiant efforts of these facilities, they cannot provide enough health services for illegal aliens. Hospitals complain bitterly about their inability to serve more indigent patients.

The issue of adequate healthcare for illegal aliens must be viewed from the perspective of the current cohort of immigrant aged and younger undocumented immigrants. If these younger individuals do not currently receive adequate care, they will die in middle age or become an aged population with poor health status and a high prevalence of chronic conditions. Probably the largest age group among illegal aliens comprises individuals now in their 30s and 40s who will reach old age during the same period as the baby boomers. Early in the next century it will be much more costly to provide healthcare for conditions that could be prevented by adequate healthcare now.

SUMMARY AND CONCLUSIONS

During this century, the 8 million immigrants who arrived in the United States during the 1980s is second in numbers only to the 8.8 million immigrants who arrived between 1900 and 1910 (Vobedja,1990). Because of the diversity of current and future immigrants, elders of the future will represent a new challenge for all service providers. This challenge will occur with greater certainty as Congress recently voted to raise the immigration quota and allow immigration from countries not formerly represented in large numbers in the United States.

The number of older people from this wide range of countries can also be expected to swell once illegals who obtained amnesty under the Immigration Reform and Control Act become U.S. citizens. These new citizens can apply to have their parents enter the country under the first immigration preference of family reunification.

Human-service providers and the aging network must become equipped to deal with the rich tapestry of elders they will be asked to serve during the next century. Strategies must now be developed to meet the challenge posed by the growing diversity among immigrant and ethnic minority aged.

REFERENCES

Baker, S., 1990. *The Cautious Welcome*. Washington, D.C.: The RAND Corporation and The Urban Institute, Program for Research on Immigration Policy.

Barresi, C., 1987. "Ethnic Aging and the Life Course." In D. Gelfand and C. Barresi, eds., *Ethnic Dimensions of Aging*. New York: Springer.

Gelfand, D.,1988. "Maryland Legalization Applicants: Program Utilization Analysis." Baltimore: University of Maryland School of Social Work.

Gelfand, D., 1989. "Immigration, Aging and Intergenerational Relationships." *Gerontologist* 29:366–72.

Hahn, R. A. et al., 1990. "Excess Deaths from Nine Chronic Diseases in the United States, 1986." *Journal of the American Medical Association* 264: 2654–59.

Lipson L. G. and Kato-Palmer, S. 1988. "Asian Americans." *Diabetes Forecast* 41: 48–51.

Morioka-Douglas, N., 1990. *Aging and Health: Asian/Pacific Island Elders*, Stanford Geriatric Education Center Working Paper Series, no. 3, Ethnogeriatric Reviews. Stanford, Calif.: Stanford Geriatric Education Center, Stanford University.

Tong, A., 1991. "Eating Habits of Elderly Vietnamese in the United States." *Journal of Nutrition for the Elderly* 10(2): 35–48.

Vobedja, B., 1990. "U.S. Growth in 1980s Fueled by Immigrants." *Washington Post*, December 31, p. 4.

Vobedja, B.,1991. "Asian, Hispanic Numbers in U.S. Soared in 1980s, Census Reveals." *Washington Post*, March 11, p. 5.

Yano, K., Reed, D. M. and Kagan, A., 1985. "Coronary Heart Disease, Hypertension and Stroke among Japanese-American Men in Hawaii: The Honolulu Heart Program." *Hawaii Medical Journal* 44: 297–325.

Yee, B. W. K., 1989. "Loss of One's Homeland and Culture During the Middle Years." In R. A. Kalish, ed., *Coping With the Losses of Middle Age*. Newbury Park, Calif.: Sage.

Yee, B. W. K., 1990a. "Health and Mental Health Risks, Beliefs, and Practices of Vietnamese Adults." Galveston: University of Texas Medical Branch.

Yee, B. W. K., 1990b. *Variations in Aging: Older Minorities, Second Edition.* Curriculum Module, Texas Consortium of Geriatric Education Centers, University of Texas Medical Branch at Galveston, US DHHS Grant #5-D31-AH66005-05, Bureau of Health Professions.

Yee, B. W. K., in press. "Markers of Successful Aging Among Southeast Asian Refugees." *Women and Therapy* 12(2).

Chapter 3

Gerontology and the Relevance of Diversity

E. Percil Stanford and Donna L. Yee

As an academic discipline and professional area of work, gerontology is very new; it thus has the advantage and disadvantage of having thrust upon it the uncertainties that accompany modern social and technological change. Gerontology must bear the burden of manifesting all the positives that the developments in modern social science and knowledge have to offer. For this reason alone, there is a clear mandate for gerontology in the nineties and beyond to accurately reflect a diverse society.

Policy issues will continue to become more complex as conscious efforts are made to be more comprehensive and inclusive when addressing needs of older people. Social policy in gerontology has historically emanated from research based on predominantly Anglo male populations. Policy restructuring based on diverse populations is needed at all governmental levels. Gerontology may set the tone or provide the standards for bringing about diversity in human service disciplines and professions.

GERONTOLOGY AND 'MINORITY' POPULATIONS

Research about the aged and aging, particularly with regard to projected demographic trends, shows that the white "majority" will soon become one of several "minority" groups in several states. The fastest growth in the number of persons over 65 is occurring in non-white, particularly Hispanic and Asian American, populations. We will no longer be able to assume that gerontology in the United States is about an essentially white, relatively homogeneous population. As a fledgling discipline, gerontology's first step in knowledge building has logically been to adhere to the first empirical principle of science: the observation and definition of normal distributions in the aging and aged population. In many ways, studies of the aged overall placed the 10 percent or 5 percent of each nonwhite population on the margin of these studies. Broad descriptive studies, which looked for similarities rather than differences among the aged, need to concentrate equally on differences and to highlight mutual trends.

In the last three decades, an amazing growth of information about the aged and the aging process has led to many new theories about the ways in which social and economic status affect the quality of life for individual aged and their family caregivers (Barer and Johnson, 1990; George and Gwyther, 1986; U.S. Congress, 1987). These ideas about how problems are defined and addressed have been the basis for much social policy development, and most of these studies include few "minority" respondents. As a result, for example, our perceptions about respite care as an intervention to support and sustain informal caregiving efforts for persons who are chronically ill focus less on the types of competing burdens and the social and economic contexts of caregiving demands. Studies appear to define respite care as short-term relief of long-term caregiving demands, and pilot programs focus on intact families with limited competing demands on the primary caregiver's time, strength, and emotional energy (Lawton et al.,1989; Zarit et al., 1986). Perspectives like those of Gibson (1990), Die and Seelbach (1988), Sung (1990), and Yip (1990) add new dimensions to the context in which other populations would define respite, understand a respite service, and use it if it were available and affordable.

In many respects, research findings that apply to the majority population are not useful when practitioners are trying to understand how issues like caregiver burden affect target populations (Hernandez, 1991). Journal articles and editorials by established "minority" researchers such as James Jackson, Manuel Miranda, Kyriakos Markides, and Jersey Liang have outlined several theoretical, design, and methodological issues that must be addressed when designing and conducting studies of target populations (Jackson, 1989; Markides et al., 1990; Miranda and Kitano, 1986). The issues they outline, together with the need to incorporate careful sampling approaches related to target populations, are major challenges for "minority" gerontology in the next decade.

While not "representative," the large existing body of research that includes small nonrepresentative samples should not be overlooked (Biafora and Longino, 1990; Center for Intergenerational Learning, 1988; Die and Seelbach, 1988; Gibson, 1990; Jiobu, 1988; Johnson and Barer, 1990; Montero, 1981; Nee and Wong, 1985; Nguyen et al., 1980; Tran, 1990; Watson, 1984). Exploratory and descriptive studies will continue to be necessary to bolster our understanding of the breadth and scope of diversity within and across target populations. Unfortunately, many smaller populations have been defined by comparison with the majority population (e.g., African Americans were compared to whites with regard to socioeconomic status, use of services, service need, and patterns of informal caregiving and support) (Council on Ethical and Judicial Affairs, 1990; Council on Scientific Affairs, 1991; Espino et al., 1988; U.S. Department of Health and Human Services, 1985; U.S. Department of Health and Human Services, Public Health Service, 1990).

Comparisons of blacks to whites relative to health status and access to healthcare imply that minorities need to "catch up" to whites. The context is hierarchical— one group is ahead. In some ways significant research comparisons suffer from an effort to draw conclusions about "minority" populations, because such comparisons are grounded in an assumption of a "majority" standard (for level of education, savings needed to maintain lifestyle in retirement, willingness to provide intergenerational caregiving, etc.). Knowledge about "minority" populations was not acquired in the context of the experiences and behavior of discrete population groups. Studies that compare recently immigrated Korean elders with Korean elders in the United States for more than one generation are seen as interesting, but only to a special interest group of (mostly "minority") researchers (Sung, 1990).

Efforts to launch large studies that might address issues of the "minority" American population, because they could offer new theories or perspectives about the way the "majority" population ages, have only begun to receive government and academic support. In initial cross-national studies conducted in the 1980s, some Asian countries (Japan, China, Taiwan) were compared with Western countries (European and North American) regarding their need to develop aging and long-term-care policies (Schulz and Davis-Friedmann, 1987). Japan's recognition as a country with the fastest growing number of aged among "developed" world countries is significant here, as much because comparisons are being made across racial, ethnic, and cultural lines as because the comparisons are across economic systems.

EMPIRICAL CONSIDERATIONS

Gerontological research in the past three decades has successfully broadened our understanding of aging as part of human development and of the aged population in our society. We not only understand how older persons differ from other age groups and from one another with regard to economic and social status, but we also are beginning to understand that issues such as economic security, healthcare and health status, and well-being might be defined differently among an increasing proportion of racial and ethnic subgroups of older persons (Taeuber, 1990). While rates of morbidity and mortality seem to have improved for the aged in general over the last 10 years, and as more elders are able to adopt healthier lifestyles that result in fewer days with disabilities, these trends are not as persistently true for African Americans, Hispanics, Asian Americans and Pacific Islanders, American Indians and Alaskan Natives, and persons with disabilities (U.S. Department of Health and Human Services, Public Health Service, 1990). The 1990 census is challenging us to recognize the growing diversity of the aged population—nationally, regionally, and locally—and how that diversity is often correlated with accessing the benefits of longer, healthier lives for the aged in our society.

With the exception of a few efforts such as the 1979 National Survey of Black Americans, research about racial and ethnic groups within the larger population has been confined to "special interest" and "small area" studies. Because the samples of persons studied were not randomly chosen, the findings in these studies cannot be considered representative of the population(s) studied. In the last decade, technological advances in statistical methods and the ability to gather large-scale nationally representative samples have reinforced an attitude that studies of specific racial and ethnic populations were not informative or were interesting only for the sake of making comparisons with the overall or majority aged population. Furthermore, because elders in most target populations are clustered regionally, statistical approaches that do not accommodate population diversity within and between regions lose critical information about factors that affect specifically targeted populations. Finally, data analyses that attempt to identify adequate subsamples of African Americans, Hispanics, Asian Americans/Pacific Islanders, and American Indians have been fraught with problems of inadequate sample size across ethnic or racial subgroups. National surveys have not consistently oversampled target populations to assure analyses of issues such as spousal impoverishment, excess disability, or levels of informal caregiving in relation to racial/cultural descriptors. Even when studies do oversample target populations, they tend to focus only on African Americans or on Hispanics, so results can only be dichotomous—couched in terms of white versus black, or Hispanic versus non-Hispanic. In a recent criticism raised about this analytic approach in studies of Hispanics published in the *Journal of the American Medical Association*, Rodolfo Eichberg (1991) and Aaron Manson (1991) presented different reasons why such dichotomous categories did not provide useful information (Ginzberg, 1991). Changes in policy to shift design and sample methodology, as well as analytical foci that better reflect the diversity of the aged population, would lead to new perspectives on issues that have an impact on the aged and aging. By incorporating the concept of population diversity into study designs, issues of race or other targeted characteristics would no longer be defined in terms of "deviance" from a "white" standard but would look at the heterogeneity of the aged population in this country. This is not to say that comparisons for mortality and morbidity, or service access and service utilization of target populations compared to whites, will not continue to be helpful in evaluating health status. It does indicate that new approaches to assessing progress on service access, service availability, and service use would benefit from models that account for heterogeneity within and between target populations. The diversity of the aged population nationally is an opportunity to expand the tools and models that are applied to understanding the status of major economic, social, and political issues in gerontology today.

Acknowledging diversity can also cause us to be overwhelmed with *differences* and discourage us from seeing the progress or lack of progress we are making in improving the quality of life of older persons. Not only do the aged have mixed income and education levels, and mixed family and primary caregiving networks, but they also have a greater mix with regard to race, language, and ethnicity that many believe significantly contributes to differences between subgroups of aged. Within many communities of ethnic minority elders, there are differences between subgroups who arrived in the United States when young and those, sponsored by grown children, who are recent arrivals; between those who remain immigrants and speak little English and those who become naturalized citizens and may speak marginally functional English; and finally, between elders who are first, second, and third generation Americans.

STRUGGLING WITH MULTICULTURALISM

A recent lead article in the *Boston Globe* (12/30/90) announced, "Multi-culturalism is becoming a way of life." The particular article discusses a rich diversity of popular music in America now written, performed, and often produced by Haitians, Cubans, Portuguese, Vietnamese, Brazilians, North and South Africans. In the same week, the same newspaper described the unresolved conflict in an upper-middle-class suburb of Boston where parents are disputing whether or not the public high school should reinstate an Advanced Placement Western Civilization course. The course apparently complemented two other Western civilization courses, and two new "non-Western" civilization courses. Parents against the reinstatement wanted both Western *and* non-Western civilization course work to meet part of the humanities requirement for graduation. Parents for the reinstatement wanted their children to take only Western civilization courses to meet the graduation requirement, because *that* was their child's cultural heritage. America is, again, at a crossroad. We can address the growing heterogeneity in this society by changing immigration quotas to encourage more white European and Western Hemisphere immigrants who will balance the large numbers of nonwhite Eastern Hemisphere immigrants now entering the United States, and we can continue to define this country as having a Judeo-Christian culture that tolerates "other" cultures. America can also acknowledge its diversity and accept the challenge to develop a new language that validates and affirms differences as an essential part of the economic and social fabric of one society. America's diversity is not a melting pot, and it may not be a "mosaic" or a "tossed salad." How our diversity will come to be characterized, named, and tolerated is as much a challenge in gerontology as in other disciplines.

MULTICULTURALISM AND GERONTOLOGY

Gerontologists who are educators, policy makers, and practitioners can join in developing a new language and a new vision that sees diversity as a positive, energizing force for understanding the aged and aging in this country. Each of us has a distinct role in shaping the pursuit of gerontological knowledge and in applying this knowledge to improve services that enhance the quality of life and living of future generations of elders. We need to reach back, to better understand "traditional" ways in which communities have defined aging and care for their aged, in order to carry a positive and caring vision of aging into the future. At the same time, we need to develop ways to accommodate technology, and we must understand the way technology changes human relationships and the way we age. Focusing on the diversity within target populations—on the "traditional" and also on the "Americanized" versions of cultural values that determine whether events are defined as problems or challenges, social burdens or role responsibilities—can provide new energy and new perspectives. The effect will be seen in our definition of problems, and in our development of solutions.

REFERENCES

Barer, B. M. and Johnson, C. L., 1990. "A Critique of the Caregiving Literature." *Gerontologist* 30(1): 26–29.

Biafora, F. A. and Longino, C. F., 1990. "Elderly Hispanic Migration in the United States." *Journal of Gerontology: Social Sciences* 45(5): S212–19.

Center for Intergenerational Learning, 1988. *Distant Branches . . . Distant Roots, a National Symposium on Older Refugees in America.* Washington, D.C.: Center for Intergenerational Learning, Temple University, June, p.15.

Council on Ethical and Judicial Affairs, 1990. "Black-White Disparities in Health Care." *Journal of the American Medical Association* 263(17): 2344–46.

Council on Scientific Affairs, 1991. "Hispanic Health in the United States." *Journal of the American Medical Association* 265(2): 248–52.

Die, A. H. and Seelbach, W. C., 1988. "Problems, Sources of Assistance, and Knowledge of Services Among Elderly Vietnamese Immigrants. *Gerontologist* 28(4): 448–52.

Eichberg, R. D., 1991. "The Health Care of Hispanics." Letters to the Editor. *Journal of the American Medical Association* 264(16):2064.

Espino, D. V. et al., 1988. "Hispanic and Non-Hispanic Elderly on Admission to the Nursing Home: A Pilot Study." *Gerontologist* 28(6): 821–24.

George, L. K. and Gwyther, L. P., 1986. "Caregiver Well-Being: A Multidimensional Examination of Family Caregivers of Demented Adults." *Gerontologist* 26(3): 253–59.

Gibson, R. C., 1990. "Minority Families as Resources for Their Elders in an Aging America: Issues for the 1990s and Beyond." In E. P. Stanford and F. Torres-Gil, eds., *Diversity in an Aging America: Challenges for the 1990s.* San Diego, Calif.: National Resource Center on Minority Aging Populations.

Ginzberg, E., 1991. "Access to Health Care for Hispanics." *Journal of the American Medical Association* 265(2): 238–41.

Hernandez, G. G., 1991. "Not So Benign Neglect: Researchers Ignore Ethnicity in Defining Family Caregiver Burden and Recommending Services." Letters to the Editor. *Gerontologist* 31(2):271–72.

Jackson, J. S., 1989. "Race, Ethnicity and Psychological Theory and Research." Guest Editorial. *Journal of Gerontology: Psychological Sciences* 44(1): P1–P2.

Jiobu, R. M., 1988. "Ethnic Hegemony and the Japanese in California." *American Sociological Review* 53(June), 353–67.

Johnson, C. L. and Barer, B. M., 1990. "Families and Networks Among Older Inner-City Blacks." *Gerontologist* 30(6): 726–33.

Lawton, M. P., Brody, E. M. and Saperstein, A. R., 1989. "A Controlled Study of Respite Service for Caregivers of Alzheimer's Patients." *Gerontologist* 29(1):8–16.

Manson, A., 1991. "The Health Care of Hispanics." Letters to the Editor. *Journal of the American Medical Association* 264 (16):2064.

Markides, K. S., Liang, J. and Jackson, J. S., 1990. "Race, Ethnicity, and Aging: Conceptual and Methodological Issues." In *Handbook of Aging and the Social Sciences.* Orlando, Fla.: Academic Press, pp. 112–29.

Miranda, M. R. and Kitano, H. H. L., eds., 1986. *Mental Health Research and Practice in Minority Communities: Development of Culturally Sensitive Training Programs.* Rockville, Md.: U.S. Department of Health and Human Services, PHS, ADAMHA, National Institute of Mental Health.

Montero, D., 1981. "The Japanese Americans: Changing Patterns of Assimilation Over Three Generations." *American Sociological Review* 46: 829–39.

Nee, V. and Wong, H., 1985. "Strength of Family Bonds in Asian American Socioeconomic Achievement." *Sociological Perspectives* 28: 281–306.

Nguyen, A., Bounthinh, T. and Mum, S., 1980. *Folk Medicine, Folk Nutrition, Superstitions.* (U.S. DOL contract #99-7-998-36-17.) Washington D.C.: TEAM Associates.

Schulz, J. H. and Davis-Friedmann, D., eds., 1987. *Aging China: Family, Economics, and Government Policies in Transition.* Washington, D.C.: Gerontological Society of America.

Sung, K.T., 1990. "A New Look at Filial Piety: Ideals and Practices of Family-centered Parent Care in Korea." *Gerontologist* 30(5): 610–17.

Taeuber, C., 1990. "Diversity: The Dramatic Reality." In S. A. Bass, E. A. Kutza and F. M. Torres-Gil, eds., *Diversity in Aging.* Glenview, Ill.: Scott, Foresman, pp. 1–45.

Tran, R. V., 1990. "Language Acculturation Among Older Vietnamese Refugee Adults." *Gerontologist* 30(1): 94-99.

U.S. Congress, 1987. *Losing a Million Minds: Confronting the Tragedy of Alzheimer's Disease and Other Dementias* (Report No. OTA-BA-323). Washington, D.C.: Office of Technology Assessment.

U.S. Department of Health and Human Services, 1985. *Report of the Secretary's Task Force on Black & Minority Health,* vol. 1. Executive Summary No. 017-090-0078-0. Washington, D.C.: U.S. Department of Health and Human Services.

U.S. Department of Health and Human Services, Public Health Service, 1990. *Healthy People 2000: National Health Promotion and Disease Prevention Objectives.* Summary

Report No. (PHS) 91-50213. Washington, D.C.: U.S. Department of Health and Human Services, Public Health Service.

Watson, W. H., ed., 1984. *Black Folk Medicine: The Therapeutic Significance of Faith and Trust.* New Brunswick, N.J.: Transaction Books.

Yip, B. C., 1990. "Cultural Changes." In E. P. Stanford and F. Torres-Gil, eds., *National Symposium on Minority Aging: Diversity in an Aging America. Challenges for the 1990's.* San Diego, Calif.: National Resource Center on Minority Aging Populations.

Zarit, S. H., Todd, P. A. and Zarit, J. M., 1986. "Subjective Burden of Husbands and Wives as Caregivers: A Longitudinal Study." *Gerontologist* 26:(3): 260–66.

Chapter 4

Entitlements:
What Do They Mean?

John H. Skinner

The concept of entitlement raises a question about how one becomes entitled to something, in this case to public benefits. Put another way, What is an entitlement and how does it relate to the concept of targeting? The definition of entitlement is the establishment of a right or claim to something, in this case to benefits. This is the denotation of the word; however, its connotation in the aging field is related to the notion of universal access to all benefits, regardless of need or income.

I would like to begin this discourse with the conceptual argument that there are at least two kinds of entitlements: earned and implied. What is the difference? Earned entitlements are those to which an individual has a legitimate claim by power of documented contributions. Implied entitlements are granted on the basis of implied contributions attributed to a group or class of people. The former are individually based while the latter are population based.

Estes (1979) indicated that "human services strategies reflect different classes of 'deservingness.'" Entitlements are one class of deservingness whereas welfare is another. If we examine the concept of entitlements in this light, we find that social programs can be rather easily categorized as (1) not an entitlement, (2) an earned entitlement, or (3) an implied entitlement. Let us first examine the concept of earned entitlement. The most obvious example is income. When one works, one is entitled to a reasonable compensation for one's services. The logic of this form of exchange theory is that there is a sense of right that validates the demands for return on one's investment (one's toil). In the case of Social Security, most workers pay a part of their income into a "retirement account"; although they have no freedom of choice in the matter, they do have the expectation that they will reap benefits when they retire. Social Security is an earned benefit to which contributors have a full right—they are entitled to receive it.

Earned entitlement is unique in that an individual claim on benefits exists, and those benefits vary according to one's contribution. Social Security is one program that would clearly qualify as an earned entitlement. If we move to the concept of an implied entitlement, we find more amorphous criteria. Implied entitlements are generally based on a population characteristic. In the case of aging programs, the population characteristic is generally a defined age. Programs that employ implied entitlements are often called universal entitlement programs. However, they are not truly universal since they actually target age as the criterion for eligibility. The entitlements for these programs are implied because they are based on assumptions—in the case of the aged, that this segment of the population has a claim. The actual claim is implied more than earned. The Older Americans Act (OAA) programs and Medicare represent examples of implied entitlements.

Let us examine each of these implied entitlements. The OAA programs are often referred to as universal entitlements. What is the basis of these entitlements? They are based on the idea that older people, as a group, have made their contributions to society and are therefore entitled to benefits. What about Medicare? Medicare is an implied entitlement since it is also driven by a population criterion, age, and a direct reference to receipt of Social Security. One does not have to prove an individual claim of contributions; that is implied by population status—being over 62 years of age—or being a recipient of Social Security retirement benefits.

Some have attempted to muddle the issues of entitlement programs by introducing issues of targeting and resource allocation. We argue that all programs are targeted to some degree. Social Security targets those in the labor market to raise the funds for those targeted to receive benefits. Elementary school education targets children; the Early Periodic Screening, Diagnosis, and Treatment program targets mothers and children; and the OAA targets older people. A distinction should be made between implied entitlements to access to program services and the actual services one may receive. In the best of all worlds, everyone would get everything he or she wanted. However, when the reality is that there is not enough funding to serve everyone, hard decisions must be made, and rationing occurs.

The role of government should be to address the needs of the most unfortunate in the society who otherwise could not help themselves. Government must provide those services that are not provided by the private sector to those people who will not be served by the private sector. Therefore, targeting within implied entitlement programs means establishing priorities for resources, according to need. The issue is not one of ethnicity, race, or minority status. Those persons in the greatest economic and social need must be given priority over those who may have access to private resources. The OAA could be organized around a two-tiered system—one that is population based, another that is based on individual needs. The greatest proportion of funds would necessarily go to individually based client services. But a portion could still be set aside to address programs and services of benefit to the entire older population. A program structured in this manner can be a universal entitlement while at the same time using targeting to assure that the most needy get the necessary services.

Recent proposals to use a means test for Social Security benefits are an affront to every working person in this country. How many people would stand by proposals to "means test" their eligibility to withdraw money from their savings account? How about means-testing how much they can receive from their employer's retirement plan, to which they contributed all their work years? Social Security is not a welfare program; it is an earned entitlement to which one must contribute to be "entitled" to withdraw. It is a gross insult to the years of hard work and contributions to begrudge anyone, regardless of income, their Social Security benefits. The Social Security system was never intended to be the sole source of income in retirement. Retirees were expected to augment their Social Security income with savings, private pensions, and investments. It would be a cruel hoax to turn the tables on those who played by the rules and penalize them for being successful. Threats to earned entitlements are much more emotionally and politically volatile than are threats to implied entitlements because of the legitimate claims that can be made on individual contributions.

REFERENCE

Estes, C. L., 1979. *The Aging Enterprise.* San Francisco: Jossey-Bass, p. 234.

Chapter 5

Targeting and Means Testing, Aging and Need

Neal E. Cutler

There is no doubt that as we approach the year 2000, *diversity* is the hallmark of our aging society. It will not come as a shock to any informed observer that a population of 30 million persons age 65-plus is very heterogeneous. But this very diversity is a challenge as well as an asset. It is no longer scientifically sufficient or politically acceptable to simply note that the older population includes people of different ethnicities, economic and social classes, or health statuses.

The policy implication of this challenge, simply stated, is that diversity does not stop at the edge of ethnic status. After all, we readily acknowledge that old people are not all alike. And we should recognize also that minority elderly are not all alike; nor are older Hispanics or older blacks or older Asians/Pacific Islanders or older Native Americans all alike. What's a policy maker to do?

Over the past 25 years, the politics of scarce resources has increasingly employed allocations based first on age and then on the needs of minority elderly. We are now coming to recognize that ethnic or minority status may not be the best—and is certainly not the only— basis for social policy. Ethnicity and need are not necessarily synonymous. Indeed the appropriate question, for both scholarship and policy, is not, Are ethnicity and the need the same? but, Under what circumstances is ethnicity a valid indicator of need?

For example, policies and programs over the past several decades have succeeded in lowering the poverty rate within the older population to the extent that, at about 12 percent, it is about the same as for the U.S. population as a whole. But clearly this "success" has been uneven: For older black women, for example, the poverty rate is closer to 55 percent. The picture is complicated even more by recent trends in minority aging, such as the pattern of acculturation and assimilation described elsewhere in this volume by Rivas and Torres-Gil.

And so we return to the basic question that all societies face: What should be the societal rules for allocating scarce resources? Let me suggest three principles that should guide any consideration of the specific rules that will be debated in this matter.

First, clearly there must be different rules for different programs and policies. Entitlements and earned benefits represent broad social contracts that we should not tamper with. By analogy, if I make annual $2,000 contributions to an Individual Retirement Account for 15 years, manage it wisely, and watch it grow to $75,000, then public policy should not later tell me that I may not receive the proceeds because I am the wrong income, age, gender, or ethnic classification.

Second, by the early 1990s we have been sufficiently exposed to policy debates over the issue of need versus age, integrated versus categorical programs. Following from the first principle, if a program is indeed a *poverty program*, then clearly financial resources should be the primary criterion for access to program benefits. Wealthy elderly should not be eligible for benefits of such programs no matter what their age, gender, or ethnic status may be.

On the other hand, we recognize full well that there are other kinds of programs whose very mission is to provide benefits for older persons as a community. The informational, identity, independence, and social interaction benefits of a neighborhood senior center, a referral service, or a community transportation system serve the needs of older persons across most of the social and economic fabric of society.

Third, from its earliest history the United States has been a *federal* nation in which the states and localities share power with the national authorities. The states came first, and so it is written in our Constitution. To be sure, federalism is neither a simple nor a fixed way of doing business. It is better characterized as a pendulum that for over 200 years swings between local/state and national authority.

And so in aging policies, as in other domains of social policy, we have programs that are national in scope and others that are designed to be responsive to the diversity across and within communities. Consequently, as a general principle for discussing the rules of allocation for scarce resources, clearly we should distinguish between centralist and federalist policies—acknowledging that the allocation rules should be different.

These principles may be applied to aging policy in the following ways:

There should be little debate that programs designed explicitly for the poor, such as Medicaid and Supplemental Security Income, are appropriately means-tested programs. Social Security clearly is more complex. The social contract suggests that I have earned those basic benefits just as I have earned my IRA, and they should not be means-tested. But cost-of-living adjustments (COLAs) may well be a different story. Why not allocate these "salary increases" progressively, on a needs-targeted basis? And at this point federalism may also be an appropriate part of the allocation rule: The COLAs could reflect regional or even local variations in the cost of living.

The Older Americans Act programs, tall in symbolism and short in budget, seem to be where the allocation debate has been most vocal. Like Medicare, Title III nutrition and social support services are a policy device for maintaining the health and independence of all aging Americans—regardless of social, ethnic, or financial status. Older Americans Act programs should not be means-tested at the individual level.

But perhaps communities should be means-tested. As a federal-state-local program, the flow of funds need not be the same for all. Communities that are more needy should receive more resources. Of course, such a mechanism is already in place: targeting. Since the late 1970s the state-to-local Planning and Service Area allocation of funds has been guided by the Intrastate Funding Formula—a kind of social-geographical means-test. Areas with greater economic or social need are supposed to receive larger allocations.

But this, of course, brings us back to the basic theme of this commentary: the interaction of diversity, ethnicity, and rules for allocation of scarce resources. Given the goals of the Older Americans Act, what should be the allocation rules?

Since the OAA is not a poverty program but does aim to provide services that are especially important to the economically needy, economic factors should be included. But there are other needs rooted in advanced age and still others suggested by the multiple jeopardies of age, ethnicity, and gender—needs that are separate from poverty and economic need.

Finally, since this a federalist program, we must recognize the responsibility of different localities to define and measure their own needs, and to design allocation rules that are responsive to the local and demographic diversity in their older populations. But federalism also defines a national legal and moral framework in which states and localities may implement their allocation rules, as the *Meek v. Martinez* federal court decision clearly indicates.

Chapter 6

Public Entitlements:
Exclusionary Beneficence

Louise Kamikawa

In the land of "our" forefathers the notion of class has traditionally been and continues to be an overriding consideration in public policy formation. With its roots in the Northeast, this orientation—and the underlying belief system about how peoples coexist—is woven into the fabric of our social contract; class is implicitly assumed to be the major factor affecting all public and private spheres of living.

While more than a grain of truth exists in this hypothesis—and it certainly did apply in eighteenth century New England—it is anachronistic to continue to allow the subtle application of "classism" to permeate public policy in the United States of today. The focus on class—traditionally and certainly in the latter part of this century—has obviated the necessity to consider color as an essential variable in the formulation of public policy. Class and color often function in tandem with each other, but the idea that they are the same is an illusion.

In the last four decades, the elderly population has grown exponentially, outpacing any other segment of our society. This has placed greater demands on government, requiring that policy makers reevaluate the needs of this particular population. The risks and vulnerabilities incurred with old age have generated greater demands for public service/welfare measures. Government has had to assume an increased protective role. Correspondingly, the expenditures for the elderly have resulted in the "graying of the federal budget" (Hudson,

1978; Califano, 1978; Samuelson, 1987). With the expenditures to the elderly representing a major component of all social welfare expenditures (McMillan and Bixby, 1980), public resistance and criticism have been mounting.

The combination of class-rooted public policy orientation and the recent developments regarding the elderly raises some important issues, particularly as they relate to older minorities:

1. How are beneficiaries of government intervention defined?
2. Are benefits based on need?
3. What is the impact of needs- and nonneeds-based benefits on older minorities?

This chapter theorizes that public policy currently targets benefits for the elderly by class and serves as "an intervening variable to ensure status maintenance in old age" (Nelson, 1982). Moreover, using class as a public policy mechanism serves to exclude consideration of minority populations.

SOCIAL CLASS, RACE, AND AGING

There is a pervading belief that all the variables of old age are experienced fairly uniformly and that seniority is the demarcation line beyond which all class and status attainment variables become moot. Class variables such as family origin, education, occupational attainment, and income are all examined (Sewell and Hauser, 1975) to define an individual's status, but only to the point of his or her seniority. More alarming is that the status attainment literature on people of color is sparse and obscure and often treated as undifferentiated information, relegating its use to a limited audience. The outcome of the lack of attention to social status and stratification of the elderly is to objectify them as a social class unto themselves, thus obscuring social and economic inequalities and further exacerbating the relative negative status of people of color. Henretta and Campbell (1976) examined income variation among the elderly, finding that the factors that determine income differences are the same before and after retirement. The effect of attainment variables on income are not reduced in old age, negating the posture that all persons experience the impact of aging evenly. Studies conducted by various minority organizations (Pacific/Asian Elderly Research Project, 1977; Lacayo, 1980, for the Asociación Nacional Pro Personas Mayores; National Indian Council on Aging, 1980) not only document the disparate impact of attainment variables on older minorities but suggest that these variables have a worsening effect on that segment of the elderly population. Such variables as assets accumulation, tax policies, health insurance measures, pension policies, and other governmental interventions have served to ensure the persistence of social class differences into old age (Henretta and Campbell, 1976).

Social welfare measures for the elderly parallel those welfare measures for nonelderly, attributing approved and disapproved classes of public dependency (Titmuss, 1965). "Approved" classes receive entitlements as a right resulting from preretirement occupational status, i.e., health insurance, private pensions, Social Security, income transfers such as tax protected retirement savings, property tax relief, and tax exemptions. "Disapproved" classes receive benefits as a measurement of "paternalism" (Friedman, 1962), not right. Such programs generally are means-tested and provide a "minimal level of care and sustenance" (Nelson, 1980).

ENTITLEMENTS: CLASS VERSUS RACE

Although the needs of various segments of the elderly population are quite different and access to resources to meet the needs uneven, very little is done to discriminate need within the population. Since social provisions are determined by socioeconomic status, the inequalities experienced in preretirement years are sustained.

Entitlement benefits/programs, composed primarily of income maintenance interventions, are the mainstay of public efforts to support the elderly. Nelson (1980), in his analysis of benefits to the elderly, conceptualizes a three-tiered network of benefits for this population. He also identifies three separate and distinct groups of elderly recipients of these benefits/programs.

Poor Elders' Benefits

The first tier is composed of means-tested welfare programs, which are directed to the poorest or "marginal elderly" class (Nelson, 1980). These programs are the most invasive in establishing participation eligibility, punitive in their treatment of participants, and complex in their requirements. The continuum of benefits/programs includes Supplemental Security Income (SSI), Medicaid, Title XX, and Food Stamps.

The needs of the "marginal" elderly are absolute; many remain poor even after receiving public income transfers. The data show that minorities, women, single persons, and "old" old are disproportionately represented in this group (Tissue, 1977). Even after the passage of SSI, those older persons living at or above the poverty line had increased only 6 percent between 1973 and 1984.

The healthcare program for the poor is Medicaid, also means-tested. Thirty percent of Medicaid expenditures are directed to the poor elderly, primarily for institutional care (Nelson, 1980). The provision of service is uneven and limited. Medicaid falls under state jurisdiction, with some states like Arizona opting to formulate their own health program. Expenditures vary by states, as do the regulations, creating unevenness in the service system. The bias toward institutional care limits outlays for other medical interventions; in 1978 1 percent of all Medicaid expenditures went to home health services (General Accounting Office, 1991). The elderly poor paid more in out-of-pocket costs for healthcare than did nonelderly poor (Feder and Holahan, 1979).

Title XX of the Social Security Administration (SSA) provides the mainstay of social services to the poor, "marginal" elderly. Their participation in the Older Americans Act (OAA) programs has been minimal; the primary beneficiaries of OAA programs have been nonpoor, white, lower-middle/middle-class elderly (Estes and Newcomer, 1978). Further, when the programming has been targeted to the poor, the participation rate of minorities has been minimal and far below levels necessary to address the needs of the particular group.

Lower-Middle- and Middle-Class Elders' Benefits

This second tier includes both lower-middle class and middle class; there is a perceived need based on relative deprivation as opposed to the objective need experienced by the poor elderly (Townsend, 1973). With the onset of old age and retirement, they attempt to maintain their preretirement middle-class lifestyle and do so through public support. This group relies primarily on earnings-related Social Security benefits, Medicare, and the OAA program. Other private resources are minimal, generally limited to savings. Without Social Security, approximately 60 percent would fall below the poverty threshold (Ball, 1978).

All programs targeted for this class are assumed to be integrative, either improving or maintaining the standard of living and status that recipients had during their working years. Service interventions seek either to reintegrate the individual or compensate him or her for losses in linkages to the community and resources. Individual beneficiaries perceive services as a right, and the system responds to that perception.

Social Security and Medicare require no arduous or extensive eligibility process and no income or assets tests are applied. This group is not perceived to be a welfare class with the ascribed stigmas. It is apparent in their utilization patterns of Medicare; in 1970 the National Opinion Research Center reported that per capita Medicare expenditures were approximately 70 percent higher for elderly with incomes above $11,000 than for those with incomes below $6,000. The per capita outlays for hospital costs are twice as high for high-income groups than low-income groups (Davis and Schoen, 1977). Physician visits commensurately increase with income. This parallels service utilization patterns of those individuals prior to their retirement.

Middle- and Upper-Middle-Class Elders' Benefits

Nelson (1980) refers to this tier as the integrated class. This group not only receives government-supported pensions, they also have private pensions, assets, and income and benefits from favorable tax policies. They are able to maintain the socioeconomic status they had during their preretirement years. With such status, they retain the roles and community relationships necessary for social integration.

Healthcare coverage is comprehensive for this class and ensures optimum availability and access to necessary services. This is provided at the cost of Medicare and Medicaid patients, as physicians and hospitals will limit Medicaid/Medicare patients to serve higher-paying, private insurance patients. It must also be noted that private insurance subscribers are provided tax subsidies that undergird their ability to pay higher costs, serving to raise healthcare costs generally (Greenspan and Vogel, 1980).

BENEFITS: CLASS VS. RACE

The application of class as a measure of analyzing public policy is a necessary, but not a sufficient, criterion for ensuring appropriateness and adequacy of intervention mechanisms for all elderly. It assumes homogeneity of experience, perception, and participation in, and benefit from, the full spectrum and hierarchy of institutions and resources. Clearly, for people of color, who are disproportionately represented among the poor and disenfranchised, the use of class as a sole criterion serves to deny access to goods and services as it assumes a similarity of color and class. Minority status implicitly places groups outside the structure as separate entities. They are treated differentially and again access to class status on a fragmented basis, as reflected in our national educational crisis and our employment practices in the social order.

Public policy measures directed at the elderly clearly demonstrate this phenomenon; even in programs for the poor/marginal class, the representation of minorities is far less than their reported objective needs would indicate. Census figures show that in 1989 over 30 percent of all blacks over 65, 20 percent of Hispanics, and 14.5 percent of Pacific/Asians were poor, yet they represent less than 3 percent of all poverty programs for the elderly. Ten percent of older whites were poor in 1989, yet they consume 97 percent of those benefits outlays for the poor. For non-means-tested programs such as those of the OAA, the picture has been more severe. Programs with no income or asset tests have most consistently served all classes of white populations. Class allows the illusion that everyone is being served because the poor are included in the system. But the resources are provided from a white perspective incorporating majority values and behaviors, relegating the minority population to a position of nonalignment and nonmembership. Moreover, service providers, predominantly white, are unable to adapt or to reconcile differences brought about by minority participation and therefore create exclusionary programs, ones allowing the status quo. As a result, minorities have been consistently underserved in the OAA programs. It has taken legislative mandates and litigation to rectify the low participation rate of minorities. Policy makers and service providers have not provided leadership in their efforts. It has taken efforts within minority groups to have an impact on the system and bring about change. But reliance on such efforts is both shortsighted and self-defeating vis-à-vis the public policy infrastructure.

PUBLIC BENEFITS INTEGRATION

A benefit structure based on political and subjective entitlement standards like class is not effective for all older persons. Such a structure has a serious negative impact on people of color, irrespective of their "class" standing. We can no longer abide by the hypothesis that class participation cross-cuts races. We do not have a monolithic universe of older persons. Therefore, a structure that identifies minority status as a measure for determining public policy interventions must be instituted. The objective need of all minority groups must be delineated and appropriate service measures created, and these measures must be monitored and evaluated. With the perceived limitation of resources, it will be necessary to address the needs of the most needy if we are to ensure quality maintenance for all. The high degree of deterioration of certain populations in this country is too closely paralleling what is seen in under-developed countries.

It may be necessary to consider a guaranteed annual income, a national healthcare program, and a reconsideration of tax policies that now favor high-income beneficiaries. We cannot continue a policy of "benign neglect"; it is becoming an observable and metastasizing cancer.

REFERENCES

Ball, R., 1978. *Social Security Today and Tomorrow*. New York: Columbia University Press.

Califano, J., 1978. "U.S. Policy for the Aging—A Commitment to Ourselves." *National Journal* 10: 1575–81.

Davis, K. and Schoen, C. *Health and the War on Poverty*. Washington, D.C.: Brookings Institution.

Estes, C. and Newcomber, R., 1978. *State Units on Aging Discretionary Policy and Action in Eight States*. San Francisco: Administration on Aging Report.

Feder, J. and Holahan, J., 1979. *Financing Health Care for the Elderly*. Washington, D.C.: Urban Institute.

Friedman, M., 1962. *Capitalism and Freedom*. Chicago: University of Chicago Press.

General Accounting Office, 1991. "Minority Participation in AoA Programs." Washington, D.C.: Subcommittee on Aging. Senate Testimony.

Henretta, J. and Campbell, R., 1976. "States Attainment and States Maintenance: A Study of Stratification in Old Age." *American Sociological Review* 41: 981–92.

Hudson, R., 1978. "The Graying of the Federal Budget and Its Consequences for Old Age Policy." *Gerontologist* 18: 428–40.

Lacayo, C. G., 1980. *A National Study to Assess the Service Needs of the Hispanic Elderly*. Los Angeles, Calif.: Asociación Nacional Pro Personas Mayores.

McMillan, A. and Bixby, A., 1980. "Social Welfare Expenditures, Fiscal 1978." *Social Security Bulletin* 35: 746–57.

National Indian Council on Aging, 1980. *Needs Assessment in Older American Indians*. Albuquerque, N.M.

Nelson, G., 1980. "Contrasting Service to the Aged." *Social Service Review* 54: 376–89.

Pacific/Asian Elderly Research Project, 1977. *Critical Factors in Service Delivery: Preliminary Findings.* Los Angeles, Calif.

Samuelson, R., 1987. "The Elderly: Who Will Support Them?" *National Journal* 10: 1712–17.

Sewell, W. H. and Hauser, R. M., 1975. *Education, Occupation and Earnings: Achievement in the Early Career.* New York: Academic Press.

Tissue, T., 1977. "The Effect of SSI on the Life Situation of the Aged." San Francisco: National Gerontological Society. Paper.

Titmuss, R., 1965. "The Role of Redistribution in Social Policy." *Social Security Bulletin* 28: 14-20.

Townsend, P., 1973. *The Social Minorities.* London: Allen Lane.

Chapter 7

Psychosocial Correlates of Health and Illness Among Minority Elders*

Neal Krause and Linda A. Wray

As reported in academic journals and the popular press, today's elderly are a highly heterogeneous group, a virtual "symphony of cultural diversity" (Bass et al., 1990, p. v). Many policy makers and healthcare providers are familiar with data illustrating wide differences across the elderly in health status, income levels, educational attainment, marital status, and living arrangements. However, they are often less familiar with even more marked differences across and among the rapidly growing populations of ethnic minority elderly. A greater understanding of the essential reasons for and implications of both similarities and differences is crucial to effective healthcare delivery.

For example, while federal programs have improved the health and economic status of the average elderly person in recent years, "the transition to a social policy that supports a vital and productive old age is still occurring in an alarmingly *uneven* fashion" (Bass et al., 1990, p. iv). A look beyond the mean illustrates that minority elders remain among the most economically disadvantaged and chronically ill in society and the most in need of social support and health services (see,

*Support for preparation of this article was provided by National Institute on Aging grant RO1 AG-08491 and the National Resource Center on Minority Aging Populations, funded by Administration on Aging grant 90-AM-0339.

among others, Lacayo, 1980; Trevino and Moss, 1984; Jackson, 1988; Jackson and Perry, 1989; Commonwealth Fund Commission, 1989; National Center for Health Statistics, 1990). What is more, it appears that factors that influence health status may differ for white and nonwhite elders. Unfortunately, high-quality research on these factors remains limited (see Jackson, 1988, for a discussion of this problem).

This chapter selectively reviews research that addresses just one component of the healthcare debate—how psychosocial factors, particularly social supports, are linked to health and illness. Older blacks and Hispanics are emphasized in this discussion simply because of space limits and the dearth of rigorous research on social supports and older adults in other ethnic and cultural groups. First, psychosocial correlates of illness are outlined and mortality differences across racial groups are examined to illustrate the importance of social supports for the health of ethnic minority elderly. Second, issues relating to life expectancy are identified. Finally, research methods and policy implications are discussed.

SOCIAL SUPPORTS AND HEALTH STATUS

Social supports may play a major unifying role in health maintenance during later life (e.g., House et al., 1988) by buffering or reducing the deleterious effects of stressful life events on health, promoting positive health behaviors, and fostering use of informal as well as formal healthcare services. In effect, these supports may influence the onset and progression of illness and recovery from it (Cohen, 1988).

For example, while older adults who are exposed to stressful life events are more likely to experience subsequent health problems than are elderly people who have not confronted significant life stress, the adverse effects of the stress may be reduced for older adults with strong social support systems (see Markides and Cooper, 1989, for recent reviews of this research). In one of the few studies that examine stress and social supports among older adults of color, Gibson and Jackson (1987) found that adequate social support systems among black elders appear to reduce the negative effects of stress on physical limitations.

Past studies on ethnicity and health in later life have focused on bivariate relationships between race, age, gender, and various measures of health status (e.g., Jackson and Perry, 1989; Markides et al., 1989). Although contributing invaluably to the literature, the studies reveal little about why and how race or ethnicity are related to health separate from other biological, environmental, socioeconomic, or cultural factors. Studies on the interface between stress and social support may help provide answers to these important questions.

Proponents of the differential exposure hypothesis contend that older minority group members are at greater risk for developing physical health problems because they are exposed to a greater number of stressful experiences (e.g., social and economic discrimination and language barriers) than are members of the majority (Krause, 1990a). If this is the case, then health-related problems of the minority elderly may be understood more clearly if research focuses on stressors associated with disadvantaged social position (Markides and Lee, 1990).

The social-supports research suggests that elders from ethnic minority groups may have stronger social support systems, especially with respect to kinship ties, than do older whites (Antonucci, 1985; Markides and Mindel, 1987). The strength of one's support systems may partially account for one's differential exposure and response to stress (Kessler, 1979; Ulbrich and Warheit, 1989).

Emerging research suggests that a one-to-one correspondence does not exist between ethnicity and familial support or stressors (Taylor et al., 1990; Chen, 1991). By illustrating that race is only imperfectly related to social supports and stress, and subsequently linking stress and support with health outcomes, researchers may speculate more clearly on the relationship between heterogeneous ethnic minority groups and illness (Gibson and Jackson, 1987).

Social Supports and Health Practices

Health status can be assessed by examining causes of mortality. Age-adjusted mortality rates by cause show that blacks are more likely than whites to die from heart diseases, malignant neoplasms, diabetes, accidents, and homicides (Markides and Mindel, 1987; Jackson and Perry, 1989; National Center for Health Statistics, 1990). In contrast, Hispanics living in the Southwestern United States have lower age-adjusted mortality rates from heart disease and malignant neoplasms than do white non-Hispanics. However, when compared to both blacks and whites, Hispanics have higher mortality rates from infective and parasitic diseases as well as diabetes. In addition, deaths from AIDS and hypertension disproportionately affect both Hispanics and blacks relative to whites (National Center for Health Statistics, 1990).

Many of these health problems can either be avoided altogether or modified through medical, rehabilitative, or lifestyle interventions.

For example, ethnic and racial disadvantage for some health problems may result from underutilization of screening for the prevention and early detection of diseases (Kravitz et al., 1990; Solis et al., 1990; Harlan et al., 1991). In addition, social supports may promote such positive health practices as good diet and exercise, as well as screening, in turn lowering the risk of developing certain debilitating conditions.

High rates of obesity and diabetes are characteristic of economically disadvantaged populations. Obesity is a powerful risk factor for diabetes among older blacks and Hispanics (Markides and Mindel, 1987; Lieberman, 1988; Markides et al., 1989) and may also be related to hypertension in the black elderly (Anderson, 1988). Diabetes and hypertension are two of the leading causes of death among older blacks and Hispanics.

Hispanics are generally more obese and less physically active than white non-Hispanics, are less likely to participate in lifestyles that promote cardiovascular health, and are two to five times more likely to have diabetes than the general U.S. population (Stern et al., 1983; Hazuda et al., 1983; Hanis, et al., 1985; National Center for Health Statistics, 1990). However, because obesity alone does not explain the high rates of diabetes among older Mexican Americans, other factors such as genetics must be considered as well (Stern et al., 1983).

Given the supposition that obesity, diabetes, and hypertension may manifest the same underlying disease process (Donahue et al., 1990), unraveling these factors may help to predict, prevent, or postpone complications and develop appropriate interventions (Markides et al., 1989).

Social supports and dietary practices may be linked. Older adults often rely on supportive relationships for transportation to the grocery store, for meal preparation, for mealtime companionship, and for information on recipes, diet, and the healthfulness of foods (McIntosh, et al., 1989). Unfortunately, studies that examine associations between social supports and nutrition, positive health behaviors, and health status among minority elders are currently limited (Anderson et al., 1987), but such research may identify important relationships.

Social Supports and Healthcare Use

Social supports, in the form of informal caregiving and formal mechanisms to foster awareness of available healthcare services, may affect the progress of and recovery from disease (Cohen, 1988; Krause, 1990a). For example, greater contact by older Cuban Americans with their relatives is associated with increased awareness of social services and, in turn, with greater social service utilization (Starrett et al., 1989). Mindel and Wright (1982) also report that greater contact with kin is related to increased service use among older blacks, although not among elderly whites. These studies support the hypothesis that informal support systems serve as links between the formal healthcare system and minority elders with health problems (Krause, 1990a).

In contrast, Chapleski (1989) suggests that strong kinship ties may instead reduce awareness of formal services because informal network members substitute for that care. In fact, the potentially important substitution of informal for formal healthcare services may be more likely to occur among older blacks. Whether the linking or the substitution hypothesis proves to be the more accurate predictor of behavior, it remains clear that informal networks play an important role in healthcare delivery to older adults of color.

LIFE EXPECTANCY

Further, research on racial differences in life expectancy raises additional healthcare planning issues. Since the turn of the twentieth century, life expectancy has improved dramatically—although not evenly—across minority and majority groups (Kitigawa and Hauser, 1973). The data also reveal an interesting trend among older blacks. At age 65, whites are expected to live longer than blacks, but around age 75 the trend reverses, and blacks appear to have more remaining years than whites.

Researchers speculate that this change in life expectancy (known as the mortality crossover effect) reflects a "selective survival" in which the least robust persons in minority groups die at earlier ages and relatively hardy minority elders survive to older ages (Markides and Mindel, 1987). In contrast, a mortality crossover does not appear to occur between Hispanics and white non-Hispanics.

Cardiovascular diseases contribute significantly to the mortality crossover phenomenon (Nam et al., 1978). While higher rates of hypertension may explain the higher mortality rates from heart disease suffered by middle-aged blacks relative to their white counterparts (Markides and Mindel, 1987), the data are inconsistent in explaining the apparent Hispanic advantage (Markides et al., 1989).

Some researchers suggest that the mortality crossover effect, and selective survival, may be altered by improvements in the overall economic status of older blacks (Markides and Mindel, 1987). Recent data showing that the proportion of nonwhites living below the poverty level has declined steadily since 1965 (Chen, 1991), with corresponding improvements in mortality rates, suggest that the proportion of middle-aged blacks surviving to older ages may increase in the future if economic status improves.

However, available data also indicate that ethnic minorities have a higher prevalence of chronic disabling conditions than do white elderly (e.g., Trevino and Moss, 1984; Mehdizadeh and Taylor, 1990), and the chronic conditions are appearing at younger ages for ethnic minorities than they are for whites (Crimmins et al., 1987).

Thus, the economic and demographic trends—suggesting there will be many more aged minorities, with more of them living to advanced old age—coupled with the findings that they may experience greater and earlier disability with increased longevity than is usual among whites, may in turn place increasing demands on informal and formal support systems (Krause, 1990b; Wray, 1991).

POLICY IMPLICATIONS

A host of research issues come into play whenever health and ethnicity are examined. Among them are difficulties in defining and measuring ethnic or minority status (Markides and Mindel, 1987); recognizing significant intra- and intergroup similarities and differences (Wray, 1991); and measuring health status (Anderson et al., 1987), social support (Krause, 1988), and stressful life events (Krause, 1990c).

In addition, because much of the available research on ethnic and minority groups is based on cross-sectional rather than longitudinal data, more is known about current cohorts of older and younger populations at a specific time than is known about their aging across the life course. Other data problems include a relative lack of culturally appropriate questionnaires, a lack of comparability across research, and small regional samples that compromise generalizability (Markides and Mindel, 1987; Delgado et al., 1990).

For these reasons, proposals that aim to accommodate the changing needs imposed by an increasingly diverse population are somewhat speculative. Rigorous empirical data must separate out the effects of race and ethnicity from other biological, socioeconomic, environmental, and cultural factors in order to understand how social supports are associated with health and illness. Such data are crucial to developing and implementing policies that will increase healthcare coverage and utilization of services and improve the health status for all members of society.

Available data suggest that because minority and ethnic elderly tend to be disadvantaged relative to their white counterparts on measures of life expectancy, health status, and mortality and morbidity rates, they tend to have a greater per capita need for healthcare services. To the extent that ethnic minority elderly remain disproportionately among the poor and near-poor, recent policy changes (e.g., increased Medicare deductibles and cost-sharing) have raised the "cost" of publicly funded healthcare. Privately funded healthcare is often out of financial reach (Smeeding, 1986).

Because their work histories and citizenship status may have precluded jobs covered by Social Security and Medicare, ethnic minority elderly may be less adequately insured than are other elderly. For example, Hispanics are less likely than the general population to have health insurance coverage and a routine place for healthcare (Commonwealth Fund Commission, 1989; Solis et al., 1990).

But even those who may have some healthcare coverage are not guaranteed adequate healthcare. For many older persons—particularly the older old, ethnic minorities, and women living alone—out-of-pocket healthcare expenses are stressful, depleting meager resources, putting people at risk of poverty, and often forcing the choice of accepting Medicaid or going without any healthcare at all (Minkler and Stone, 1985; Warlick, 1985; Burkhauser and Duncan, 1988; Coe, 1988; Dressel, 1988; Holden, 1988).

In addition, at older ages, minorities tend to rely on informal supports for their care. And most older persons, whether minority or nonminority, prefer the use of home- or community-based long-term-care services to institution-based services, yet the latter tend to dominate current healthcare policies and programs. Given this preference and the lack of noninstitutional long-term-care benefits, families with limited resources who choose to care for their elderly at home may be particularly burdened economically.

Healthcare policy must be enhanced in order for programs to more effectively serve populations in need. Enhancements might include requiring "diversity assessments" of existing and proposed policies to identify barriers and evaluate programs in terms of their impact on ethnic minorities (Torres-Gil, 1990 in Wray, 1991)(see also Capitman et al., this issue).

For example, healthcare data indicate that more rather than fewer older persons are remaining at home and are returning home earlier after a major illness and that the prevalence of chronic rather than acute conditions increases with age (Verbrugge, 1984, 1989). Sociological data show that minority populations have benefited from increased life expectancy but remain at a disadvantage relative to nonminorities, that minorities have greater rates and earlier onset of disabling conditions, and that ethnic minority elders have historically been cared for in home environments to a greater extent than have nonminority elderly. Other data suggest that differential opportunity costs and language barriers may partially account for healthcare locus differences (Headen, 1990; Solis et al., 1990).

A diversity assessment of the existing healthcare delivery system might result in recommending (1) a move away from the traditional institution-based acute-care model and toward a flexible, affordable, and accessible community- or home-based chronic-care model (U.S. House of Representatives, 1989), and (2) use of functional rather than chronological age as a measure of eligibility for health and social benefits. In addition, public policy may be revised to increase incentives to provide and consume culturally and linguistically sensitive health promotion, prevention, and chronic-care services targeted to those most in need (e.g., Weeks and Cuellar, 1981; Lubben and Becerra, 1987; Kravitz et al., 1990; Lee and Markides, 1991).

CONCLUSION

Bass and colleagues (1990) contend the following:

> [Even] as it may liberate, diversity also complicates. It calls upon society to exhibit a greater sensitivity and responsiveness to the needs of older individuals who vary widely in all dimensions . . . [and] flexibility on the part of our social institutions (p. 183).

Thus, demographic, socioeconomic, health status, healthcare utilization, and psychosocial data demonstrating the rapid growth and diversity of elderly minority and ethnic groups have long-term implications for healthcare policies in the United States. Current public policies designed for a homogeneous population made up of white, English-speaking elders with like needs are increasingly obsolete. Looking ahead, how do we eliminate the obstacles handicapping many ethnic and minority elderly and provide access to adequate and appropriate healthcare?

First, further rigorous research is critical. Researchers must discern the effects of race or ethnicity—separate from other biological, environmental, socioeconomic, or cultural factors—on social supports, health behavior, and health status. Second, providers, minority aging organizations, and minority elders must take more active responsibility for articulating their concerns and relevant research findings to policy makers.

Third, policy makers must understand and acknowledge the implications of an increasingly diverse society and determine what will constitute adequate and appropriate healthcare within continuing fiscal constraints. Finally, methods of program planning, implementation, and evaluation must be revised to meet future needs effectively and efficiently.

REFERENCES

Anderson, N. B., 1988. "Aging and Hypertension among Blacks: A Multi-dimensional Perspective." In J. S. Jackson, ed., *The Black American Elderly: Research on Physical and Psychosocial Health.* New York: Springer.

Anderson, R. M., Mullner, R. M. and Cornelius, L. J., 1987. "Black-White Differences in Health Status: Methods or Substance?" *Milbank Quarterly* 65: 72–99.

Antonucci, T. C., 1985. "Personal Characteristics, Social Support and Social Behavior." In R.H. Binstock and E. Shanas, eds., *Handbook of Aging and the Social Sciences.* New York: Van Nostrand Reinhold.

Bass, S. A., Kutza, E. A. and Torres-Gil, F. M., eds., 1990. *Diversity in Aging.* Glenview, Ill.: Scott, Foresman.

Burkhauser, R. V. and Duncan, G. J., 1988. "Life Events, Public Policy, and the Economic Vulnerability of Children and the Elderly." In J. Palmer, T. Smeeding and B. Torrey, eds., *The Vulnerable.* Washington, D.C.: Urban Institute Press.

Chapleski, E. E., 1989. "Determinants of Knowledge of Services to the Elderly: Are Strong Ties Enabling or Inhibiting?" *Gerontologist* 29: 539–45.

Chen, Y. P., 1991. "Income Status of the Elderly by Race and Ethnicity." Paper presented at the Gerontological Society of America Minority Aging Research Agenda Meeting, Airlie, Va.

Coe, R. D., 1988. "A Longitudinal Examination of Poverty in the Elderly Years." *Gerontologist* 28(4):540–44.

Cohen, S., 1988. "Psychosocial Models of the Role of Social Support in the Etiology of Physical Disease." *Health Psychology* 7: 269–97.

Commonwealth Fund Commission, 1989. *Poverty and Poor Health Among Elderly Hispanic Americans.* Baltimore, Md.: Commonwealth Fund Commission.

Crimmins, E. M., Saito, Y. and Ingegneri, D. G., 1987. "Changes in Life Expectancy and Disability-Free Life Expectancy in the United States." *Population and Development Review* 15: 235–67.

Delgado, J. L. et al., 1990. "Hispanic Health and Nutrition Examination Survey: Methodological Considerations." *American Journal of Public Health* 80 (Supplement): 6–10.

Donahue, R. P. et al., 1990. "Hyperinsulinemia and Elevated Blood Pressure: Cause, Confounder, or Coincidence?" *American Journal of Epidemiology* 132: 827–36.

Dressel, P. L., 1988. "Gender, Race, and Class: Beyond the Feminization of Poverty in Later Life." *Gerontologist* 28(2): 177–80.

Gibson, R. C. and Jackson, J. S., 1987. "The Health, Physical Functioning, and Informal Support of the Black Elderly." *Milbank Quarterly* 65: 421–54.

Hanis, C., Ferrell, R. E. and Schull, W. J., 1985. "Hypertension and Sources of Blood Pressure Variability Among Mexican Americans in Starr County, Texas." *International Journal of Epidemiology* 14: 231–38.

Harlan, L. C., Bernstein, A. B. and Kessler, L. G., 1991. "Cervical Cancer Screening: Who is Not Screened and Why?" *American Journal of Public Health* 81(7): 885–90.

Hazuda, H. P. et al., 1983. "Ethnic Differences in Health Knowledge and Behaviors Related to the Prevention and Treatment of Coronary Heart Disease: The San Antonio Heart Study." *American Journal of Epidemiology* 117: 717–28.

Headen, A. E., 1990. "Opportunity Cost of Time and Black/White Differences in Nursing Home Use." Paper presented at the 1990 Annual Meeting of the Gerontological Society of America, Boston, Mass.

Holden, K. C., 1988. "Poverty and Living Arrangements Among Older Women: Are Changes in Economic Well-Being Underestimated?" *Journals of Gerontology: Social Sciences* 53(1): S22–S27.

House, J. S., Landis, K. R. and Umberson, D., 1988. "Social Relationships and Health." *Science* 241: 540–45.

Jackson, J. J., 1988. "Social Determinants of the Health of Aging Black Populations in the United States." In J. S. Jackson, ed., *The Black American Elderly: Research on Physical and Psychosocial Health.* New York: Springer.

Jackson, J. J. and Perry, C., 1989. "Physical Health Conditions of Middle-Aged and Aged Blacks." In K. S. Markides, ed., *Aging and Health: Perspectives on Gender, Race, Ethnicity, and Class.* Newbury Park, Calif.: Sage.

Kessler, R. C., 1979. "Stress, Social Status, and Psychological Distress." *Journal of Health and Social Behavior* 20: 259–72.

Kitigawa, E. and Hauser, P., 1973. *Differential Mortality in the United States: A Study in Socioeconomic Epidemiology.* Cambridge, Mass.: Harvard University Press.

Krause, N., 1988. "Gender and Ethnicity Differences in Psychological Well-Being." In G. L. Maddox and M. P. Lawton, eds., *Annual Review of Gerontology and Geriatrics,* vol. 8. New York: Springer.

Krause, N., 1990a. "Illness Behavior in Later Life." In R. H. Binstock and L. K. George, eds., *Handbook of Aging and the Social Sciences.* New York: Academic Press.

Krause, N., 1990b. "Perceived Health Problems, Formal/Informal Support, and Life Satisfaction Among Older Adults." *Journals of Gerontology: Social Sciences* 45: S193–S205.

Krause, N., 1990c. "Measuring Life Stress." *Stress Medicine* 6: 201–8.

Kravitz, S. L., Pelaez, M. B. and Rothman, M. B., 1990. "Delivering Services to Elders: Responsiveness to Populations in Need." In S. A. Bass, E. A. Kutza and F. M. Torres-Gil, eds., *Diversity in Aging.* Glenview, Ill.: Scott, Foresman.

Lacayo, C. G., 1980. *A National Study to Assess the Service Needs of the Hispanic Elderly—Final Report.* Los Angeles, Calif.: Asociación Nacional Pro Personas Mayores.

Lee, D. J. and Markides, K. S., 1991. "Health Behaviors, Risk Factors, and Health Indicators Associated with Cigarette Use in Mexican Americans: Results from the Hispanic HANES." *American Journal of Public Health* 81(7): 859–64.

Lieberman, L. S., 1988. "Diabetes and Hypertension among Blacks: A Multidimensional Perspective." In J. S. Jackson, ed., *The Black American Elderly.* New York: Springer.

Lubben, J. E. and Becerra, R. M., 1987. "Social Support Among Black, Mexican, and Chinese Elderly." In D. E. Gelfand and C. M. Barresi, eds., *Ethnic Dimensions of Aging.* New York: Springer.

Markides, K. S. and Mindel, C. H., 1987. *Aging and Ethnicity.* Newbury Park, Calif.: Sage.

Markides, K. S. and Cooper, C. L., 1989. *Aging, Stress, and Health.* Chichester, England: Wiley.

Markides, K. S., Coreil, J. and Rogers, L. P., 1989. "Aging and Health Among Southwestern Hispanics." In K. S. Markides, ed., *Aging and Health: Perspectives on Gender, Race, Ethnicity, and Class.* Newbury Park, Calif.: Sage.

Markides, K. S. and Lee, D. J.. 1990. "Predictors of Well-Being and Functioning in Older Mexican Americans and Anglos: An Eight-Year Follow-up." *Journals of Gerontology: Social Sciences* 45(1): S69–S73.

McIntosh, W. A., Shifflet, P. A. and Picou, J. S., 1989. "Social Support, Stressful Events, Strain, Dietary Intake, and the Elderly." *Medical Care* 27: 140–53.

Mehdizadeh, S. and Taylor, S., 1990. "Comparison of the Extent of Disability Among Older Black and White Population." Poster session presented at the 1990 Annual Meeting of the Gerontological Society of America, Boston, Mass.

Mindel, C. H. and Wright, R., 1982. "The Use of Social Services by Black and White Elderly: The Role of Social Support Systems." *Journal of Gerontological Social Work* 4: 107–20.

Minkler, M. and Stone, R., 1985. "The Feminization of Poverty and Older Women." *Gerontologist* 25(4): 351–57.

Nam, C. B., Weatherby, N. L. and Ockay, K. A., 1978. "Causes of Death Which Contribute to the Mortality Crossover Effect." *Social Biology* 25(4): 306–14.

National Center for Health Statistics, 1990. *Health, United States, 1989.* Hyattsville, Md.: Public Health Service.

Smeeding, T. M., 1986. "Nonmoney Income and the Elderly: The Case of the Tweeners." *Journal of Policy Analysis and Management* 5(4): 707–24.

Solis, J. M. et al., 1990. "Acculturation, Access to Care, and Use of Preventive Services by Hispanics: Findings from HHANES 1982–84." *American Journal of Public Health* 80 (Supplement): 11–19.

Starrett, R. A. et al., 1989. "The Cuban Elderly and Their Service Use." *Journal of Applied Gerontology* 8: 69–85.

Stern, M. P. et al., 1983. "Does Obesity Explain Excess Prevalence of Diabetes Among Mexican-Americans: Results of the San Antonio Heart Survey." *Diabetologica* 24: 272–77.

Taylor, R. J. et al., 1990. "Developments in Research on Black Families: A Decade Review." *Journal of Marriage and the Family* 52: 993–1014.

Trevino, F. M. and Moss, A. J., 1984. "Health Indicators for Hispanic, Black, and White Americans." *Vital and Health Statistics.* Series 10, No. 148. Washington, D.C.: U.S. Public Health Service, National Center for Health Statistics.

Ulbrich, P. M. and Warheit, G. J., 1989. "Social Support, Stress, and Psychological Distress Among Older Black and White Adults." *Journal of Aging and Health* 1: 286–305.

U.S. House of Representatives, 1987. *The Status of the Black Elderly in the United States.* Comm. Pub. No. 100–622. Washington, D.C.: Government Printing Office.

U.S. House of Representatives, 1988. *Demographic Characteristics of the Older Hispanic Population.* Comm. Pub. No. 100–696. Washington, D.C.: Government Printing Office.

U.S. House of Representatives, 1989. *Expansion of Community-Based Services to Special Populations.* Comm. Pub. No. 101–725. Washington, D.C.: Government Printing Office.

Verbrugge, L. M., 1984. "Longer Life but Worsening Health? Trends in Health and Mortality of Middle-Aged and Older Persons." *Milbank Quarterly* 62(3): 475–519.

Verbrugge, L. M., 1989. "Recent, Present, and Future Health of American Adults." *Annual Review of Public Health* 10: 333–61.

Warlick, J. L., 1985. "Why Is Poverty After 65 a Women's Problem?" *Journal of Gerontology* 40(6): 751–57.

Weeks, J. and Cuellar, J., 1981. "The Role of Family Members in the Helping Networks of Older People." *Gerontologist* 21: 388–94.

Wray, L. A., 1991. "Public Policy Implications of an Ethnically Diverse Elderly Population." *Journal of Cross-Cultural Gerontology* 6: 243–57.

Chapter 8

The Health, Labor Force, and Retirement Experiences of Aging Minorities

Rose C. Gibson and Cheryl J. Burns

What is in store for the work and retirement lives of minority elderly of the future? This chapter makes several speculations based on the current experiences of minorities in three closely related areas—health, work, and retirement. If the present looks bleak, it can only signal a grim future if younger and middle-aged minorities continue to have limited access to quality healthcare, good education, and effective job-training programs.

First, minority-nonminority group disparities in health and in work disability are discussed. Second, differences in the labor force experiences of minorities and nonminorities are examined. Differences in retirement experiences are identified next, followed by suggestions for new research on and interventions into the health, work, and retirement lives of minorities across the lifespan. We focus on African, Puerto Rican, Cuban, and Mexican Americans, and we recognize the need for analyzing Native Americans (Redhorse, 1981; Manson and Callaway, 1985), on whom data and research are sparse (Gelfand and Barresi, 1987).

HEALTH AND WORK DISABILITY

African, Puerto Rican, Cuban, and Mexican Americans have poorer health and more work disability than do white Americans. African and Puerto Rican Americans are the least healthy of the four minority groups (Lacayo, 1980; Trevino and Moss, 1984; Markides, 1989).

Among all ages in the civilian noninstitutionalized U.S. population from 1978 to 1980, about 14 percent of whites, Cubans, and Mexicans had activity limitation due to chronic conditions (age-adjusted) (U.S. National Center for Health Statistics, 1984). In contrast, fully 18 percent of African Americans and 19 percent of Puerto Rican Americans had limitation. Among currently employed persons aged 17 and over during the same time period, whites had about seven days of bed disability per person per year, Mexican Americans about six, Cuban Americans eight, African Americans nine, and Puerto Rican Americans 13. Similarly, whites had about five days of work loss per person per year, Cuban and Mexican Americans about four, and African and Puerto Rican Americans about eight. Of all persons with activity limitation due to chronic conditions, about 11 percent of white and Puerto Rican Americans were limited in their major activity. About 7 percent of Mexican, 12 percent of African, and 14 percent of Cuban Americans were so limited.

At midlife (ages 45–64), about 23 percent of white Americans, Cuban Americans, and Mexican Americans had activity limitation due to chronic conditions. In contrast, fully 32 percent of African and 30 percent of Puerto Rican Americans had limitation. Middle-aged whites had about eight days of bed disability per person per year in 1978–1980, Mexican Americans had about 10, Cuban Americans nine, African Americans 14, and Puerto Rican Americans 20.

White Americans aged 45–64 lost about five days of work per person per year because of poor health, Cuban and Mexican Americans about six, African Americans eight, and Puerto Rican Americans 11. Eighteen percent of middle-aged white and Mexican Americans were limited in their major activity because of chronic conditions, contrasted with 24 percent of Puerto Rican, 27 percent of African, and 20 percent of Cuban Americans.

The poorer health and greater work disability of minorities, both earlier in life and at midlife, play large parts in their disadvantaged labor force and retirement experiences.

LABOR FORCE EXPERIENCES

While minority workers are gaining importance in the labor force, they are more disadvantaged there than are nonminority workers (Borjas and Tienda, 1985). African, Puerto Rican, and Mexican Americans are the most disadvantaged of the minority groups.

In 1989 about 63 percent of the white, Mexican, and Cuban American populations aged 16 and over were employed, compared with only 56 percent of African and 51 percent of Puerto Rican Americans (U.S. Bureau of the Census, 1990a). Whites also made up the smallest proportion of the unemployed labor force (about 5 percent), while African Americans made up fully 12 percent, Mexican and Puerto Rican Americans 9 percent, and Cuban Americans 5 percent.

These minority-nonminority disparities continued on into midlife. Between ages 45 and 64, African and Hispanic Americans composed larger proportions of the unemployed labor force than did white Americans: 5.5, 5.9, and 3.1 percent, respectively (U.S. Bureau of Labor Statistics, 1989). These simple labor force statistics, however, obscure other minority-majority group differences such as the greater tendencies for minorities to be part-year, part-time, and seasonal workers or to be discouraged workers who are not even counted in labor force statistics. "Undocumented" workers further complicate labor force data on minorities because these individuals are highly mobile and only temporarily in the country (Hayes-Bautista, 1986; Sotomayor, 1986).

Lower placement in the occupational structure plays a large part in minorities' discontinuous and disadvantaged work patterns. While fully 28 percent of whites (U.S. Bureau of Labor Statistics, 1991) and 25 percent of Cuban Americans are professional and managerial, only 16 percent of African Americans (U.S. Bureau of Labor Statistics, 1991), 11 percent of Puerto Rican Americans and 9 percent of Mexican Americans are (U.S. Bureau of the Census, 1990c). Thirty-two percent of whites are in technical, sales, and clerical occupations, in contrast to 29 percent of African Americans, 22 percent of Puerto Rican Americans, 25 percent of Cuban Americans and only 12 percent of Mexican Americans. Twelve percent of whites are craftsmen, 10 percent of African Americans, 20 percent of Puerto Ricans Americans, 15 percent of Cuban Americans, and 20 percent of Mexican Americans. Finally, 14 percent of whites are laborers, contrasted with 22 percent of African Americans, 25 percent of Puerto Rican Americans, 22 percent of Cuban Americans, and fully 31 percent of Mexican Americans.

Lower levels of educational attainment (U.S. Bureau of the Census, 1990b, 1990c), discrimination in the marketplace, and language and cultural barriers contribute to minority workers' overrepresentation in the lower occupational strata (Torres-Gil, 1986). This concentration of minority workers in occupations characterized by seasonal, part-year, and part-time work denies them opportunities for job training and other programs that would promote occupational mobility. For example, black youth are underrepresented in vocational training programs and overrepresented in training courses geared toward jobs with low wages, low upward mobility, and for which there is low demand. Less than 15 percent of electronics students are black, in contrast to 65 percent of textile production students (Swinton, 1986).

Thus, the work experiences of minorities are shaped not only by their work disability, but also by their lower education and occupation levels and by the lack of opportunities for job training and advancement. These detrimental labor force experiences in youth and middle age contribute, in turn, to the unfavorable retirement experiences of minorities in old age.

RETIREMENT EXPERIENCES

Lower-level occupations and wages and more sporadic work patterns over a lifetime are leading causes of minorities' low levels of retirement income. Compared with those of whites the total retirement income packages of minorities contain larger proportions of Social Security and Supplemental Security Income (SSI) and smaller proportions of private pensions, savings, investments, and other assets. Thus, minorities are more dependent on public funds in retirement. The highly touted three-legged stool of retirement income—Social Security, savings, and private pensions—is more like a one-legged stool for many minority elderly.

Despite the greater dependence of minorities on Social Security, about 93 percent of whites aged 65 or older received Social Security in 1987, compared with only 88 percent of African Americans and 85 percent of Mexican, 74 percent of Puerto Rican, and 66 percent of Cuban Americans (U.S. Congress, 1988; 1989).

In 1987, Social Security made up about 40 percent of the total income package of older white Americans. For African and Hispanic Americans, however, Social Security made up about 57 percent and 51 percent, respectively (U.S. Congress, 1988).

Private retirement pensions were received by 33 percent of whites, 21 percent of African Americans, and only 16 percent of Hispanics. Twenty-six percent of whites, 7 percent of African Americans, and 10 percent of Hispanics received income from dividends, rents, or estates. Fully 70 percent of whites received interest income, while only 27 percent of African and 31 percent of Hispanic Americans did (U.S. Congress, 1988).

Quite in contrast, 19 percent of African Americans; 20 percent of Hispanics, and only 4 percent of whites received SSI. Thirty-six percent of the Mexican American poor received SSI, 48 percent of the Puerto Rican poor, and 46 percent of the Cuban poor (U.S. Congress, 1989). As Cuellar and Weeks (1980) point out, not all minorities who need SSI receive it. According to Lacayo (1980), Puerto Ricans are the likeliest of the three Hispanic groups to receive disability pay under Social Security (9 percent of Mexican, 12 percent of Puerto Rican, and 5 percent of Cuban Americans do).

To this point, we have shown that present cohorts of minorities are more disadvantaged than their nonminority counterparts in health, labor force, and retirement experiences—a characteristic that could be true of several more minority elderly generations to come if no action is taken. Ameliorative strategies, however, need to be based on sound research in the areas of health, work, and retirement. We turn now to some suggestions for that research.

NEW RESEARCH ON HEALTH, WORK, AND RETIREMENT

Health

Minority-nonminority group comparisons are often based on self-reports of health from subjects in national surveys. The issue is whether these reports mean the same, or are measured the same, for minorities as for nonminorities. For example, subjective interpretations of health were found to be less valid for blacks than for whites, and the measurement error in a chronic-conditions indicator was larger for whites than blacks (Gibson, 1991a). Work disability reported by subjects themselves is also less valid for blacks than for whites (Chirikos and Nestel, 1983). Attempts should be made to replicate this "Gibson Model of Self-Reported Health" with other minority groups as subjects so that minority-nonminority differences can be identified and adjusted for. Such adjustments are critical if differences in structure and measurement are not to be misconstrued as real minority-nonminority differences in self-reported health and work disability.

Counterintuitively, an older age group (75–79) in the African American population was found to be healthier and more able than a younger age group (65–74). When race comparisons were made, the African American "health handicap" was smaller in the age 75–79 than in the 65–74 group. These odd age-by-race disparities suggest adverse mortality selection processes (Gibson, 1991c) and are referred to as the "Gibson Gap." The gap also was identified by David Espino (1988) in comparisons among Mexican Americans. Since this gap has implications for the ability of various minority age groups to engage in work and other productive activity in old age, it should be explored in other minority group comparisons. For example, is the gap related to use of healthcare services and participation in postretirement work and job retraining programs by certain age groups of minority elderly?

Labor Force Experiences

Work patterns, and factors determining those work patterns, were found to be different for African American and white men and women (Gibson, 1983). In a longitudinal analysis of the Panel Study of Income Dynamics (Morgan and Duncan, 1968–present) over a six-year period, black women were found to be the likeliest of the four race and gender groups to have disadvantaged work patterns: they had been with their present employers the shortest time and had worked the fewest years, weeks, and hours per week. Those black women who were *better* educated, who received transfer income, who were older, and who lived in areas of high unemployment experienced the most discontinuous work patterns. Poor health was more consistently related to sporadic work for white men than for the other three groups. Are there similar differences in the work patterns, and the factors that predict them, when other minority groups are compared with the majority group? How might these minority-nonminority differences in work patterns be associated with minority-nonminority differences in retirement patterns? Are additional years of education also deterrents to employment for other minority women?

Retirement Experiences

Current procedural definitions of retirement may cause disadvantaged minorities to drop through the cracks in retirement research. The result could be a lack of representation of the individuals who are most in need of remedial retirement policy. One group of individuals screened out of the major retirement research today, by definition, are the "unretired-retired." These are older African Americans who look retired but do not call themselves retired (Gibson, 1987). Zsembek and Singer (1990), examining Gibson's concept of the "unretired-retired" as applied to Mexican Americans, found that health and disability played different roles in retirement depending on the definition of retirement that was used. New research should identify the "unretired-retired" in other minority groups. How might procedural definitions of retirement be changed to include these individuals in national retirement studies?

Among African Americans, the failure to adopt a retired identity was predicted by a preference for the disabled-worker role and by economic need for disability pay (Gibson, 1991b). Does this "Gibson Model of Subjective Retirement" hold in the case of other minority groups? Do disability and the availability of disability pay propel other disadvantaged minority individuals toward the disabled-worker identity and away from the retired identity?

Retirement patterns, and the factors that determine them, appear to be different for whites, African Americans, and Mexican Americans. Early retirement is more prevalent among African Americans (Gibson, 1982) and Mexican Americans (Stanford et al., 1991) than among whites. The factors that predict this early labor force withdrawal also differ. Do the same differences in early retirement, and its determinants, exist between the majority group and other minority groups, such as Puerto Ricans and Native Americans?

Research that compares minority and nonminority groups on postretirement experiences also is needed. Social and psychological factors seem to soften the effects of economic stress on the well-being of older African Americans (Gibson and Jackson, 1988) and older Mexican Americans (Dowd and Bengtson, 1978). Are such relationships among economic stress, psychosocial buffers, and well-being evident in other disadvantaged minority groups in retirement?

New research also should begin to compare minorities and non-minorities on the causal patterns among poor health and handicapping labor force and retirement experiences. The conjunctions and disjunctions of these three factors should be monitored over time. Finally, minority aging research needs to devote much more attention to concepts, measures, and methods in order to develop an intellectual core of knowledge about the health, work, and retirement of minorities as they age (Bengtson, 1979; Bastida, 1987; Gibson, 1989; Jackson, 1989; Markides et al., 1990).

IDEAS FOR INTERVENTION

It goes without saying, of course, that the well-being of future cohorts of minority elderly depends on access to better jobs, better healthcare (Jackson et al., in press), better education, and better training programs in youth and middle age. For minority elderly who already are retired, there is a need to retrain those who wish (or find it necessary) to return to work. A long-standing problem, however, is that the skills of older minorities do not keep pace with the skills needed for the new available jobs. Nor are jobs that would accommodate the greater work disability of minorities available (Gibson, 1986a; 1986b).

Malcom S. Cohen (1991) of the University of Michigan Institute of Labor and Industrial Relations (1991) puts it well: There are too many butchers, meat cutters, rail transport workers, and stenographers for the available jobs, while there are not enough college professors, computer systems analysts, and legal assistants. Educational and job-training programs for minority youth and retraining programs for minority elderly should be informed by accurate and thorough analyses of the job market.

Linguistic and cultural barriers, however, deter service use by minorities and must be prime considerations in the design of services and programs (Maldonado, 1975; Becerra, 1983; Wright et al., 1983; Valle, 1983; Torres-Gil, 1986; Harel et al., 1987).

As indicated earlier, minorities rely more than nonminorities on public funds in old age. Any program revisions that result in reduced funds will, then, affect the retirement of minorities more negatively. For example, raising the age of eligibility for Social Security benefits from age 65 to 67 means that minorities who retire early will have to wait longer after labor force withdrawal for these benefits to begin (Stanford, et al., 1991). What is more, the shorter lifespans of minorities mean they will collect Social Security benefits for a shorter period of time. These two issues raise the question of whether eligibility for benefits should be based on functional age rather than on chronological age.

African and Puerto Rican Americans often have been at the bottom when minorities were ranked on measure of health, work, and retirement. Special attention needs to be devoted to these especially disadvantaged groups—and to Native Americans—in future research, planning, programs, and services.

In summary, the poorer health and the more disadvantaged labor force and retirement experiences of present cohorts of minorities do not bode well for future cohorts of minority elderly. In the absence of more effective social intervention, these negative experiences could characterize minority elderly cohorts on into the twenty-first century—and beyond.

REFERENCES

Bastida, E., 1987. "Issues of Conceptual Discourse in Ethnic Research and Practice." In D. E. Gelfand and C. M. Barresi, eds., *Ethnic Dimensions of Aging.* New York: Springer.

Becerra, R., 1983. "The Mexican American: Aging in a Changing Culture." In R. McNeely and J. Colen, eds., *Aging in Minority Groups.* Beverly Hills, Calif.: Sage.

Bengtson, V. L., 1979. "Ethnicity and Aging: Problems and Issues in Current Social Science Inquiry." In D. Gelfand and A. Kutzik, eds., *Ethnicity and Aging: Theory, Research, and Policy.* New York: Springer.

Borjas, G. and Tienda, M., eds., 1985. *Hispanics in the U.S. Economy.* Orlando, Fla.: Academic Press.

Chirikos, T. N and Nestel, G., 1983. *Economic Aspects of Self-Reported Work Disability.* Columbus: Center for Human Resource Research, Ohio State University.

Cohen, M. S., 1991. Quoted in G. Fuchsberg, "Despite Layoffs, Firms Find Some Jobs Hard to Fill." *New York Times,* Jan. 22.

Cuellar, J. and Weeks, J., 1980. *Minority Elderly Americans: The Assessment of Needs and Equitable Receipt of Public Benefits as a Prototype for Area Agencies on Aging, Final Report.* San Diego, Calif.: Allied Home Health Association.

Dowd, J. J. and Bengtson, V. L., 1978. "Aging in Minority Populations: An Examination of the Double Jeopardy Hypothesis." *Journal of Gerontology* 33:427–36.

Espino, D., 1988. "Older Mexican-Americans." Paper presented at the annual scientific meeting of the Gerontological Society of America. San Francisco, Calif., November.

Gelfand, D. E. and Barresi, C. M., eds., 1987. *Ethnic Dimensions of Aging.* New York: Springer.

Gibson, R. C., 1991a. "Race and the Self-Reported Health of Elderly Persons." *Journal of Gerontology* 46(5).

Gibson, R. C., 1991b. "The Subjective Retirement of Black Americans." *Journal of Gerontology* 46(4).

Gibson, R. C., 1991c. "Age-by-Race Differences in the Health and Functioning of Elderly Persons." *Journal of Aging and Health* 3(3).

Gibson, R. C. 1989. "Minority Aging Research: Opportunity and Challenge." *Journal of Gerontology* 44(1).

Gibson, R. C., 1987. "Reconceptualizing Retirement for Black Americans." *Gerontologist* 27 (6).

Gibson, R. C., 1986a. *Blacks in An Aging Society.* New York: Carnegie Corporation.

Gibson, R. C. 1986b. "Blacks in an Aging Society." *Daedalus* 115(1):349–71.

Gibson, R. C., 1983. "Work Patterns of Older Black and White, Male and Female Heads of Household." *Journal of Minority Aging* 2(2).

Gibson, R. C., 1982. "Race and Sex Differences in the Work and Retirement Patterns of Older Heads of Household." *Scripps Foundation Minority Research Conference Monograph* 138–184. Oxford, Ohio: Scripps Gerontology Center.

Gibson, R. C. and Jackson, J. S., 1988. "The Health, Physical Functioning, and Informal Supports of the Black Elderly." *Milbank Memorial Fund Quarterly* 65 (supplement 2).

Hayeş-Bautista, D., 1986. "Hispanics in an Age Stratified Society." In F. Torres-Gil, ed., *Hispanics in an Aging Society.* New York: Carnegie Corporation.

Harel, Z., McKinney, E. and Williams, M., 1987. "Aging, Ethnicity, and Services: Empirical and Theoretical Perspectives." In D. E. Gelfand and C. M. Barresi, eds., 1987. *Ethnic Dimensions of Aging.* New York: Springer.

Jackson, J. S., Burns, C. J. and Gibson, R. C., in press. "An Overview of Geriatric Care in Ethnic and Racial Minority Groups." In E. Calkins et al., eds., *Practice of Geriatrics,* 2d ed. Philadelphia: W. B. Saunders.

Jackson, J., 1989. "Race, Ethnicity, and Psychological Theory and Research." *Journal of Gerontology* 44:1–2.

Lacayo, C., 1980. *A National Study to Assess the Service Needs of the Hispanic Elderly.* Los Angeles: Asociación Nacional Pro Personas Mayores.

Maldonado, D., 1975. "The Chicano Aged." *Social Work* 20:213–16.

Manson, S. and Callaway, D., 1985. *Health and Aging Among American Indians: Issues and Change for the Biobehavioral Sciences.* Unpublished monograph.

Markides, K., ed., 1989. *Aging and Health: Perspectives on Gender, Race, Ethnicity, and Class.* Newbury Park, Calif.: Sage.

Markides, K., Liang, J. and Jackson, J., 1990. "Race, Ethnicity, and Aging: Conceptual and Methodological Issues." In L. K. George and R. H. Binstock, eds., *Handbook of Aging and the Social Sciences,* 3d ed. New York: Academic Press.

Morgan J. and Duncan, G., *1968–1991. A Panel Study of Income Dynamics.* Ann Arbor: Institute for Social Research, University of Michigan.

Redhorse, J. E., 1981. "American Indian Elders: Needs and Aspirations in Institutional and Home Health Care." In E. P. Stanford, ed. *Minority Aging: Policy Issues for the 1980s.* San Diego, Calif.: Campanile.

Sotomayor, M., 1986. "Demographic Characteristics of U.S. Hispanic Populations." In F. Torres-Gil, ed., *Hispanics in an Aging Society.* New York: Carnegie Corporation.

Stanford, E. P. et al., 1991. "Early Retirement and Functional Impairment From a Multi-Ethnic Perspective." *Research on Aging* 13(1).

Swinton, D., 1986. In R. C. Gibson, ed., *Blacks in an Aging Society.* New York: Carnegie Corporation.

Torres-Gil, F., ed., 1986. *Hispanics in an Aging Society.* New York: Carnegie Corporation.

Trevino, F. M. and Moss, A. J., 1984. "Health Indicators for Hispanic, Black, and White Americans." Vital and Health Statistics, Series 10, no. 148. Washington, D.C.: U.S. Public Health Service, National Center for Health Statistics.

U.S. Bureau of the Census, 1990a. *Statistical Abstract of the United States, 1990.* Washington, D.C.: U.S. Department of Commerce, Government Printing Office.

U.S. Bureau of the Census, 1990b. *The Black Population in the United States, March 1988.* Washington, D.C.: U.S. Department of Commerce, Current Population Reports Series P-20, no. 442, Government Printing Office.

U.S. Bureau of the Census, 1990c. *The Hispanic Population in the United States, March 1989.* Washington, D.C.: U.S. Department of Commerce, Current Population Reports Series P-20, no. 444, Government Printing Office.

U.S. Bureau of Labor Statistics, 1991. *Employment and Earnings, March 1991.* Washington, D.C.: U.S. Department of Labor, vol. 38 no. 3, Government Printing Office.

U.S. Bureau of Labor Statistics, 1989. *Handbook of Labor Statistics.* Washington, D.C.: U.S. Department of Labor, Bulletin 2340, Government Printing Office.

U.S. Congress, 1988. *Demographic Characteristics of the Older Hispanic Population: A Report by the Chairman of the Select Committee on Aging, House of Representatives.* Washington, D.C.: 100th Congress, 2nd Session. Report #100-696, Government Printing Office.

U.S. Congress, 1989. *Hispanic Elderly: America's Failure to Care: Hearing Before the Select Committee on Aging, House of Representatives.* Washington, D.C.: 101st Congress, 1st Session, Government Printing Office.

U.S. National Center for Health Statistics, 1984. *Health Indicators for Hispanic, Black, and White Americans: Data From the National Health Survey.* Washington, D.C.: U.S. Department of Health and Human Services, Public Health Service 84-1576, Government Printing Office.

Valle, R., 1983. "The Demography of Mexican American Aging." In R. McNeely and J. Colen, eds., *Aging in Minority Groups.* Beverly Hills, Calif.: Sage.

Wright, R. et al., 1983. *Transcultural Perspectives in the Human Services: Organizational Issues and Trends.* Springfield, Ill.: Thomas.

Zsembek, B. A. and Singer, A., 1990. "The Problem of Defining Retirement Among Minorities: The Mexican Americans." *Gerontologist.* 30(6):749–57.

Chapter 9

Generational Equity or Interdependence?*

Meredith Minkler

In stark contrast to the "compassionate ageism" of an earlier era, which portrayed the old as weak, deserving, politically powerless, and poor, current and equally misleading stereotypes characterize the elderly as an affluent and politically powerful population group whose costly government programs are busting the federal budget (Binstock, 1985). By aggregating or "homogenizing" the old, the new stereotypes ignore the tremendous diversity within the elderly population, especially with respect to ethnicity and income. Further, such images feed into the notion that a financially comfortable population of "white old folks" is reaping generous government benefits at the expense of financially strapped workers and needy children, many of them people of color. Such juxtapositions are used by some to argue that "generational inequity," particularly in an age/race stratified society, may result in troubling age/race conflict in the years ahead (Longman, 1986; Hayes-Bautista et al., 1988).

This chapter will argue that a fundamental premise of generational equity—the notion that America's younger generations are suffering

*This chapter is based in part on a presentation to the National Symposium on Minority Aging, San Diego, Calif., June 7, 1990. An expanded version appears in M. Minkler and A. Robertson, "The Ideology of 'Age/Race Wars': Deconstructing a Social Problem," *Ageing and Society*, April 1991.

because of the elderly population and its entitlement programs—is both flawed and dangerous. At the same time, the emergence of the whole generational equity debate will be seen as a blessing in disguise to the extent that it has caused us to look more carefully at poverty in minority children and related problems that can be addressed only through broad cross-generational thinking as we begin a new decade and a new century (Kingson, 1988). The tremendous stake of the elderly and their advocates in both sides of the generational equity question will be stressed, as will the importance of changing our focus from generational equity to generational interdependence.

GENERATIONAL EQUITY AND PEOPLE OF COLOR

The concept of generational equity or "justice between generations" gained popularity in the early 1980s when a small number of journalists, academics, policy makers, and groups such as the newly formed "Americans for Generational Equity" began to argue the need for cutting back costly government entitlements for the old in order to preserve scarce resources for younger and future generations. Pointing out that the government spends six times as much on the elderly as on children, despite the fact that one in four preschoolers now live in poverty, these groups proposed a major rethinking of policies for the old in the name of justice between generations (Preston, 1984, Callahan, 1987).

But what is the truth behind the generational equity argument? Elders and their advocates have a critical dual need: first, to understand and bring to light the problems inherent in the generational equity framework, and second, to also be loud and articulate advocates for policies that better serve children, youth, and all generations.

CRITIQUING GENERATIONAL EQUITY

The logic behind the concept of generational equity can be criticized on several important counts. First, the notion that the elderly are no longer economically disadvantaged reflects an earlier mentioned tendency to homogenize the old, ignoring their tremendous diversity. The minority elderly, for example, while proportionately still small in number, are growing at a far faster rate than the white elderly. Elderly Hispanics are the fastest growing group in the elderly population, and their numbers are expected to quadruple by the year 2020 (*Older Americans Report*, 1989). Since the poverty rates of minority elders are far higher than those of whites, with, for example, 24 percent of older Hispanics and 32 percent of older blacks living below poverty line, these rapid rates of growth are particularly significant (Policy Research Associates, 1989).

Even among white elders, however, the rosy economic picture painted by proponents of generational equity is misleading. Older white women, for example, had a median income in 1987 of just $7,055 (Policy Research Associates, 1989). And among the elderly as a whole, close to 43 percent live at below 200 percent of the poverty line and hence are "economically vulnerable" (U.S. Bureau of the Census, 1985). In short, the myth of a homogeneous and financially secure elderly population block breaks down when the figures are desegregated and the true diversity of the older population is taken into account.

A second assumption underlying generational equity is the idea that working class men and women and their children—especially minority children—are suffering as a consequence of our policies and programs for the old. But a look at the real causes of the rapid upturn in poverty rates among our nation's children suggests a different explanation. Children are poor because their parents are poor (Holstein, 1989). And their parents are poor not because of entitlement programs for the old, but because of market forces that have nothing to do with elders. These forces include the following:

- A 39 percent increase in inflation during the 1980s, while the minimum wage remained the same (Brown and Gershoff, 1989).
- Significant expansions in the number of new jobs paying below minimum wage, with over half of all jobs created in the 1980s falling into this category (Home Base et al., 1989).
- A dramatic decline in the real wages of young males, which in the 1980s fell 10–20 percent below those of the 1960s (Easterlin, 1987).
- The loss of 20 million jobs in the 1980s because of plant closings and layoffs, which disproportionately affected people of color (Bluestone and Harrison, 1988).
- A dramatic rise in female-headed households, with one-fifth of all children under 6 living with single mothers in 1987 (National Center for Children in Poverty, 1990).

In short, the lowering of poverty rates in the old and the increase in poverty rates in children were caused by two very distinct sets of trends.

Still another problem with the generational equity concept lies in its assumption that the elderly alone have a stake in Social Security, Medicare, and other government programs depicted as serving only the old. That kind of depiction is unfortunate, first because it disregards the direct benefits of Social Security to younger segments of society, for example through survivor benefits, but more important because it ignores the huge indirect cross-generational benefits of such programs. By providing for the financial needs of the elderly, Social Security frees adult children from the need to provide such support directly, and in this way it reduces family financial burdens and interfamily tensions. Further, in many low-income communities of color, an elder's Supplemental Security Income or Social Security check is pooled with other family members' sources of income to enable the extended family to make ends meet.

Contrary to recent media claims, there has so far been little outcry from younger taxpayers about the high costs of Social Security and Medicare, even though many of today's young workers believe—however erroneously—that Social Security will not be there for them when they retire. A review of national opinion poll data by ethnicity further suggests that Hispanics, African Americans, and other minorities tend to be highly supportive of Social Security and Medicare and in fact are often more opposed to budget cuts in these programs than are whites, partly because such programs are more important to low-income groups in which minorities are disproportionately represented (Minkler and Robertson, 1991).

FROM GENERATIONAL EQUITY
TO INTERDEPENDENCE

In suggesting that we are not likely to see major age/race conflicts over entitlements for the elderly in the years ahead, I in no way want to imply that we can afford to be anything less than morally outraged over the high rates of poverty, illiteracy, and inadequate education, job training, and job opportunities among today's minority children and youth. The appropriate framework for mobilizing such outrage, though, is not one of generational equity but of interdependence. As Kingson (1988) has argued, such an approach to policy would create an awareness that "intergenerational competition works to the systematic disadvantage of the least powerful members of the national community" (p. 768). Generational interdependence would have us view benefits like public education and Medicare as transfers across generations that meet different needs across the life course, to the advantage of all. And it would have us create coalitions across age and ethnic lines to protect existing services and extend them to all in need.

We have seen such intergenerational thinking and advocacy around the fight for a national health program. We saw it in Miami recently, on a smaller but very important scale, when the mayor of that city gave elderly voters most of the credit for passage of a school bond initiative that would affect mainly Hispanic youth. And in Oakland, California, intergenerational thinking was reflected in the Office on Aging's decision to make itself a resource center for young as well as old, promoting intergenerational programs to address the crack cocaine epidemic. There has also been effective coalition building between groups like the Gray Panthers, AARP, and the Children's Defense Fund to protect programs and services essential across the life span.

But much remains to be done. A recent nationwide poll conducted for AARP found only 43 percent of elders agreeing that government should spend more money on public elementary and high schools (National Retired Teachers Association, 1987). Based in part on this finding, AARP is now increasing it efforts to convince members that the education of today's youth is vital to the elderly.

Such "reeducation" is critical, yet perhaps more important than convincing all elders that things like the education of youth are in the best interests of the elderly is the establishment of a new societal norm that would see the good society as, in Callahan's (1987) words, "inherently communal," rather than individual in orientation. Narrowly conceived interest-group politics would give way increasingly to a more generalized commitment to what Kingson (1988) refers to as the "equitable distribution of burdens" and shared responsibility for maintaining community and social institutions.

Minority elders and their advocates have a particular stake in such a shared vision. Minority children, young adults, and older Americans have all suffered as a consequence of the continuing effects of institutional racism and public policies that work to the disadvantage of groups that are disproportionately low income and in other ways disenfranchised.

The concept of generational interdependence is one that reminds us that a Latino preschooler in poverty, a young black mother without health insurance, and an older Chinese American living in a substandard single-room-occupancy hotel are equally a part of the socially created problem we need to confront. The national tragedy of poverty and illiteracy in our minority children cannot be blamed on our programs for the old, nor can elders and their advocates be sanguine when improvements in Social Security benefits are not accompanied by improvements in Aid to Families with Dependent Children payments and other programs aimed at the young.

The elderly and their organizations and advocates now represent one of the largest and most powerful lobbies in Washington. By working for policies and programs that better meet the needs of all ages and all ethnics groups, we have an usual opportunity for demonstrating our commitment to generational and ethnic group interdependence as a vital framework for advocacy and action in the 1990s and beyond.

REFERENCES

Binstock, R. H., 1985. "The Oldest Old: A Fresh Perspective or Compassionate Ageism Revisited?" *Milbank Memorial Fund Quarterly* 63: 420–541.

Bluestone, B. and Harrison B., 1988. *The Great U Turn: Corporate Restructuring and the Polarization of America.* New York: Basic Books.

Brown, J. L. and Gershoff, S. N. 1989. "The Paradox of Hunger and Economic Prosperity in America." *Journal of Public Health Policy* 10:425–43.

Callahan, D., 1987. *Setting Limits: Medical Goals in an Aging Society.* New York: Simon and Schuster.

Easterlin, R., 1987. "The New Age Structure of Poverty in America: Permanent or Transition?" *Population and Development Review* :195–208.

Hayes–Bautista, D., Schink, W. O. and Chapa, J., 1988. *The Burden of Support: The Young Latino Population in an Aging Society.* Palo Alto, Calif.: Stanford University Press.

Holstein, M. 1989. "Who Is Consuming Our Children?" *Generational Journal* 2(1):106–8.

Home Base, Association of Bay Area Governments and Public Advocates, 1989. "Homelessness in the Bay Area: 10 Points." San Francisco.

Kingson, E., 1988. "Generational Equity: An Unexpected Opportunity to Broaden the Politics of Aging." *Gerontologist* 28(6):765–78.

Longman, P., 1986. "Age Wars: The Coming Battle Between Young and Old." *The Futurist* 20 (1): 8–11.

Minkler M. and Robertson, A., 1991 "The Ideology of 'Age/Race Wars': Deconstructing a Social Problem." *Ageing and Society* (April).

National Center for Children in Poverty, 1990. *Five Million Children.* New York: Columbia University School of Public Health.

National Retired Teachers Association, 1987. *NRTA News Bulletin* #28, p. 2. Washington, D.C.

Older Americans Report, 1989. "Demographics and Economics." Sept. 15, p. 355. Washington, D.C.

Policy Research Associates, 1989. "Income and Poverty Status of Families and Persons in the U.S., 1984." *Consumer Income: Current Population Reports*, Series P–60, #149, Table 6.

Preston, S., 1984. "Children and the Elderly in the U.S." *Scientific American*, 25(6):44–49.

Taylor, P. 1986. "The Coming Conflict as We Soak the Young to Enrich the Old." *Washington Post*, Jan. 5, p.1.

U.S. Bureau of the Census, 1985. "Money Income and Poverty Status of Families and Persons in the U.S., 1984." *Consumer Income: Current Population Reports*, Series P–60, #149, Table 6.

Chapter 10

Young Latinos, Older Anglos, and Public Policy: Lessons from California

David E. Hayes-Bautista

The 1990 census figures for California's generations paint a picture of potential interethnic and intergenerational conflict in the very near future. The Anglo share of the population has plummeted in just 20 years. In the 1970 census, Anglos were 79 percent of the state's total population (EDD, 1986). By 1990, Anglos were only 54 percent of the state's total (Bureau of the Census, 1990) and, according to our calculations, will drop to less than 50 percent of the total population sometime in 1996.

While the Anglo proportion is shrinking, the Latino share is booming. In 1970, Latinos were truly a minority—10.9 percent of the state. By 1990, that figure had grown to 25.7 percent (Bureau of the Census, 1991), and by the year 2000 will be around 35 percent (Hayes-Bautista et al., 1988). By the time the last of the baby boom generation retires, the state's population will be around 60 percent Latino.

The reason that the Anglo population is shrinking relative to the Latino population is that Latinos as a group are over a decade *younger* than Anglos, and because of immigration and increasing fertility, are as a group actually growing younger rather than older for the time being. As the baby boomers turn 65 and swell the ranks of the elderly, the younger, working age population will increasingly be composed of Latinos.

We can see these two trends in the 1990 Current Population Survey. Put baldly, the elderly are overwhelmingly Anglo—78.1 percent of all persons age 65 and older (DOF, 1991). By way of contrast, when we consider the generation of children age 0–17, Anglos are already a minority among the young—47.9 percent. In Los Angeles County, the country's most populated, 56 percent of all births are to Latinos (LACHD, 1989), and the combination of Latino, black, and Asian births make up over 75 percent of all births.

The economy of the state is quickly and increasingly being driven by Latinos and others of the emergent (non-Anglo) majority population. Their economic success, or failure, will influence the future economic and social well-being of the largely Anglo elderly population in California.

CONDITIONS FOR CONFLICT

The shrinking Anglo population lives a world apart from the growing, youthful Latino community. Some overall indicators for 1990 present a portrait of a society perilously close to apartheid-like conditions.

Education

Anglos had an average of 13.4 years of educational attainment; Latinos had barely 9.1 years (DOF, 1991).

Income and Poverty

The Anglo population has a median family income of $43,400; Latino families earned just $26,900 (DOF, 1991). Overall, Anglos had a low rate of poverty—7.1 percent.

Even the Anglo elderly, who do experience a drop in income, nonetheless rarely experience poverty; 5.0 percent of those age 65 and over lived in poverty. In contrast, children of all ethnic groups were over four times as likely to live in poverty; 21.5 percent did so. And Latinos of all ages were the most likely of any group to live in poverty—22.0 percent (DOF, 1991).

Putting these percentages in absolute numbers will tell a story. Five times as many Latino children live in poverty (566,117) as do Anglo elderly (112,788).

On the surface, it would appear that the conditions for a very bitter interethnic and intergenerational conflict exist: a well-educated elderly

Anglo population that has rarely experienced poverty expecting to be supported in its retirement by a poorly educated, younger Latino population for which poverty is a common occurrence.

Can a conflict be avoided?

RECOGNIZING LATINO STRENGTHS

The 1990 snapshot of potential conflict need not be interpreted to mean that conflict is inevitable and unavoidable. In fact, recent research gives reason to believe that a major conflict can be avoided, if an appropriate intergenerational and interethnic compact can be developed.

Latino poverty and low education have often been interpreted as evidence of major individual, familial, and social disintegration. The model of the urban underclass does much to feed the notion that Latinos can only be a drag on the state's economy and public sector. In fact, a quick glance at some data indicate that Latinos bring tremendous strengths to the economy and the society.

High Labor-Force Participation

A key feature of the underclass model is low male labor-force participation. In 1990, Latino males had the highest labor-force participation of any group—80.8 percent compared to 76.1 percent for Anglos, 68 percent for Asian Americans, and 66 percent for blacks (DOF, 1991). This is not a recent occurrence. Census data from 1940 to 1990 show that for 50 years, Latinos have consistently had the highest labor-force participation rate *of any group* (EDD, 1980).

Low Labor-Force Desertion

The "discouraged worker" is the prototype of the urban underclass male—a person out of work for so long that he has left the labor force and no longer seeks employment. For 50 years Latinos have had the lowest rate of labor force desertion of any group (EDD, 1986).

Low Welfare Dependence

The unmarried, welfare-dependent mother is a stereotype of the underclass situation. Latinos have consistently had the lowest rate of welfare dependency of any group (DPSS, 1987).

High Family Formation

For over 50 years, Latinos have had the highest rate of family formation and the largest families.

Health

While the image of the urban underclass is of overwhelming sickness and early death, Latinos present a basic health profile that should be quite the envy of health policy makers around the country. Some key indicators from Los Angeles County (LACHD, 1989) are as follows: (1) Latinos have a life expectancy of 79.4 years, over four years longer than Anglos, who have 75.1 years. (2) Latinos have a death rate (adjusted for age) of 5.12 per 10,000, about one-third lower than the Anglo rate of 7.89. (3) The percentage of Latino babies who are of low birth weight is 5.32, compared to 5.51 percent of Anglo babies. (4) The Latino infant mortality rate was 5.7 per 1,000, less than half the Anglo rate of 11.3. (5) A recent California Field Poll showed the perhaps surprising result that Latinos drink less and smoke less than Anglos. Small area studies consistently show that Latinos use drugs less than Anglos.

Thus, while it is true that Latinos have less education, earn less, and experience poverty more than Anglos, they also exhibit considerable strength in key areas—a commitment to family and the work ethic, industriousness, and healthy behavior. And the Latino population is growing at just the right time to pick up the slack as the baby boom generation ages, retires, and leaves the labor force.

The main questions are simply these:

1. Will a labor force that is over 50 percent Latino (and about 70 percent "emergent majority") have the productive capacity to generate sufficient income and wealth to sustain the baby boom generation in its retirement?
2. Will there be a sufficient sense of societal cohesion, of singleness of purpose, to induce the large Latino working force to surrender as much as 40 percent of its payroll to fund Social Security?

These questions are being answered today by the policy decisions (or indecisions) of the Anglo population. These decisions are influenced, in large part, by Anglo perceptions of the Latino population and the effects of Latino population growth on the state and its society.

From a recently completed survey, the California Identity Project (Hayes-Bautista et al., 1991), it appears that the Anglo population is about evenly divided in its views of Latinos. We can summarize these views succinctly using the terms of "Latino-rejective" and "Latino-sensitive." About half the Anglo sample expressed a rather negative, "Latino-rejective" view of Latinos in society. In their view, Latinos conform to the underclass stereotype, and an increased Latino population will inevitably result in higher welfare costs, more unemployment and crime, increased ethnic tension, and a general worsening of conditions in society. This view is fairly well articulated by blatantly anti-Latino groups such as Light Up the Border, the Federation of Americans for Immigration Reform, and English First!.

Perhaps surprisingly, about half the Anglo population in our sample dissented from the negative view of Latinos and expressed a more positive, Latino-sensitive attitude. This half of the sample admired Latinos for their industriousness, willingness to work, strong families, and religious ties. Anglos in this group desired that their own children learn Spanish and also expressed a personal desire to learn the language. This view, unfortunately, has not yet been translated into the public discourse. There is no pro-Latino equivalent to Light Up the Border to encourage this half of the Anglo population to express its views.

Yet, this group does exist, though it may be voiceless in the public discourse on Latino policy. We would suggest that this group can most effectively activate itself to form a productive interethnic and inter-generational coalition with the growing Latino and other emergent majority populations.

A POLICY FRAMEWORK

A policy framework for Latinos in the twenty-first century does not in the least resemble the welfare policy framework of the Great Society programs of the 1960s. The new policy framework does not have to seek to compensate for weakness or deprivation; it needs only to unleash the full productive and social potential of the emergent majority. Some key areas on which to focus are labor force participation, education, and political involvement.

Labor Force Participation

The issue is not to induce Latinos to work; Latinos have always had the highest rate of labor force participation. The key is to maximize Latino contributions, but current policy seems instead to place obstacles in the way of labor force participation. Although there are many small policy-created obstacles, two in particular loom large— (1) immigration and documentation and (2) underutilization. The Immigration Reform and Control Act is an attempt to regulate away the labor force participation of undocumented Latinos. The act has failed miserably in its stated goal of discouraging immigration. It has succeeded marvelously, and perhaps unintentionally, in segregating undocumented Latino workers into the periphery of the economy, into the underground arena where many toil for long hours in unsafe conditions for below-minimum wages and without benefit of health insurance, paid holidays, workers' compensation, overtime pay, or other conditions of work most Anglos enjoy. Further, the lives of undocumented Latino immigrants can be brutally interrupted at any stage by a forced deportation. Documented immigrants and Latinos born in the United States, although technically not falling under the provisions of the Immigration Reform and Control Act, have nonetheless experienced marked increases in job discrimination and lack of job advancement by virtue of being Latino. This is because of a generalized fear on the part of employers that they *might* be undocumented.

The growing resource represented by Latino population growth is poorly utilized by major employers in the state. For one example, while Latinos are around 40 percent of the population of Los Angeles County, they are only around 8 percent of all county employees. In nearly every major organization, corporation, industry, and bureaucracy, there is a similar underutilization of Latino work energy. In the 1960s this type of underutilization was addressed via affirmative action programs. Today, such programs, while still needed, are insufficient. What is required is a new framework that will see the increased utilization of Latino talent not as a burden imposed by angry minorities, but rather as an exercise in the "administration of wealth" being offered by this growing population.

Education

The history of nearly every immigrant group has been that one generation first achieves economic mobility, then the next acquires educational attainment. Yet, in the face of this nearly universal experience (income rising first, *then* educational levels), Latinos are being told that the only way to success is to raise their educational level.

Stereotypes and fairness to one side, Latinos do willingly comply. While education has often been considered a major problem among

Latinos, the results from the California Identity Project demonstrate that Latino educational attainment is extremely responsive to public policy. In the 1950s and 1960s, when education was a priority in the state of California and the state ranked first in any number of indicators, Latino educational attainment skyrocketed: Nearly 70 percent of Latinos educated during that period graduated from high school, only slightly shy of the 80 percent graduation rate of Anglos. However, in the 1990s, California languishes near the bottom of the country in its educational efforts, making it more difficult for anyone, Latino or Anglo, to gain a decent education. For one example, the cost to students attending the University of California has risen by over 1,000 percent from 1960 to 1990.

For all the barriers, the Latino interest in education remains, and there are intact Latino families to provide support and encouragement to students. The policy objective should be to return education to its place of primacy in the state's agenda, and facilitate involvement of Latino parents in their children's education.

This is not an impossible dream. Literally all the pieces are in place on the Latino end. What is lacking is the political will to make an investment in the state's growing population of the order of magnitude that the state made in the 1950s and 1960s.

Full Political Involvement

While the state's demography changes, the state's political landscape will be controlled by the aging Anglo voter until well into the twenty-first century. This is simply a matter of demographic composition: The Latino population is disproportionately young and immigrant, two conditions that lower political participation. Nevertheless, there are many forms of political participation, particularly in the nonelectoral arena. It is in the state's interest that Latinos have a full political voice, and the Latino-sensitive Anglos can play a key role in seeing that this comes about.

THE POLITICAL FRAMEWORK

The pieces of a win-win situation are in place: a growing, younger, energetic Latino population and an Anglo population half of which would be supportive of Latino advancement. To the extent that Latinos advance, the largely Anglo elderly will have a better future.

The key step will be to forge alliances across ethnic groups and across generations. This may not be impossible. Clearly, Latinos and Anglos share some values—hard work, strong families, healthy behaviors, and the like. Even though electoral participation might be low among Latinos for the demographic reasons cited above, a combination of Latino votes, half the Anglo votes, and those of the others in the emergent majority (namely blacks and Asian Americans) could easily carry the day for an intergenerational and interethnic policy future.

A new vision of multicultural and multigenerational California needs to be developed. This vision could provide the "social glue" to bind together a multicultural population into a single society, without requiring that anyone feel diminished for being part of that larger social aggregation.

REFERENCES

Bureau of the Census, 1991. Preliminary Counts.

DOF (Department of Finance), 1991. *Current Population Survey*. Sacramento: State of California.

EDD(Employment Development Department), 1986. *Socio-Economic Trends in California, 1940–1980*. Sacramento: State of California Health and Welfare Agency.

Hayes-Bautista, D. et al., 1988. *The Burden of Support: Young Latinos in an Aging Society*. Stanford: Stanford University Press.

Hayes-Bautista, D. et al., 1991. *Redefining California: Latino Social Engagement, 1990*. Los Angeles: UCLA Chicano Studies Research Center.

DPSS (Los Angeles County Department of Public Social Services), 1987. *GAINParticipant Needs Assessment*. Los Angeles:UCLASchool of Social Welfare.

LACHD (Los Angeles County Health Department), 1989. Data Collection and Analysis.

Chapter 11

Current Trends in Living Arrangements and Social Environment Among Ethnic Minority Elderly

Carmela G. Lacayo

The explosive growth in the number of older Americans has generated a wide array of living arrangements and has increased the diversity of social environments among the elderly. It is projected that between 1990 and the year 2000, the number of households headed by a person aged 55–64 will expand from 12.3 million to 14.1 million. Households whose head is 65–74 will remain nearly static, declining from 11.6 million to 11.4 million during the decade. But the number of heads of household aged 75-plus will skyrocket from 8.7 million to 11.9 million by the turn of the century (*Housing the Elderly Report,* 1989).

Among minority elderly the rate of growth is even more dramatic. Although this article focuses mostly on the Hispanic elderly, it also illustrates characteristics common to other ethnic minorities. Between 1970 and 1980 the Hispanic older population grew by 75 percent, and the older African American population, by 34 percent. This compares to a 25 percent increase among Anglo elderly. Older Hispanics in the United States number over 2 million today, and another 1 million will be added to their number by the end of this decade.

LIVING ARRANGEMENTS:
CURRENT STATUS AND FUTURE PROSPECTS

How will rising numbers affect minority elders' living arrangements? What factors besides population growth will affect their social environment in the near and long term? Will their housing and environment increasingly resemble that of the majority elderly, or will significant differences in lifestyle between these groups persist? Answering these questions is not just a theoretical exercise. All of us—from decision makers in Washington, state capitals, and city halls, to policy makers, practitioners, and researchers in gerontology, to citizens who scarcely think about aging—have a stake in the answers. These answers will affect the lifestyle of each of us; they will determine the shape of our cities and towns and our own neighborhoods. The statistics cited above demonstrate that older people, including minority elders, will have a more and more important role in our own environment. We have a stake in caring about what their environment and living arrangements are like.

Examining the current living arrangements of minority elders will help us frame answers to the questions just posed. These arrangements are a function of income, family relationships, health status, and other factors.

Poverty is a key determinant of living arrangements. In 1988 aged Hispanics were more than twice as likely to be poor as the older Anglo population: 22.4 percent compared to 10.0 percent. Fully a third of elderly blacks (32.2 percent) lived in poverty that year (Bureau of the Census, 1989). It is no surprise that ethnic minority elders often live in substandard housing and are less likely to own their own homes than the total aged population. Homeownership among Hispanics aged 65-plus was 55.8 percent in 1983 versus 73.5 percent for all U.S. aged (Bureau of the Census, 1983). Just 61.1 percent of older blacks owned their homes at that time. Hispanic elderly men had a 56 percent probability of living in substandard housing in 1978 (Office of Policy Development and Research, 1978)—a fact later verified by the first national needs assessment of Hispanic elderly (Lacayo, 1980). Compare this to the 27 percent probability of poor housing among older Anglo men. Black aged, too, have poorer housing than the majority older population (Johnson, 1978; Rosen, 1978; Solomon, 1978; National Institute on Aging, 1980).

Martinez (1979) points out that all elders face housing problems because of decreased income at retirement, which affects ability to keep up their home, pay property taxes, or make mortgage or rent payments. But many minority elderly have struggled with these problems all their lives: Low-paying jobs not only kept them in poverty but most often provided no retirement pension. Ethnic minority elders have also had to cope with housing discrimination and "red-lining" by lending institutions, both of which have limited their housing options. Rising home-insurance costs and utility bills further jeopardize older minority homeowners' ability to retain their homes.

Keeping decent housing is an equally acute problem for older minority renters. Consider the current fair market rents for a one-bedroom apartment in Los Angeles ($618–$883), San Francisco ($758–$1,063), Chicago ($710–$851), Philadelphia ($597–$769), and Miami ($532–$711) (U.S. Department of Housing and Urban Development, 1991). A low-income older person can hardly pay such rents, especially when he or she is trying to cope with rising costs of healthcare, food, and other necessities.

If minority elderly cannot keep their homes, can they always move in with other family members? It is widely assumed that minority elders live in extended families. Some do, but most do not. The first national needs assessment of Hispanic elderly revealed that less than 10 percent have such living arrangements (Lacayo, 1980). A more recent study found that 49 percent of older Hispanics live with their spouse only, and 22 percent live alone (Commonwealth Fund Commission on Elderly People Living Alone, 1989). Older minority women living alone make up an ever rising proportion of older households. Sixty-nine percent of older black household heads living alone are women (Herbert, 1983). Fifty percent of all Japanese older households outside the West consist of just one person, and 70 percent of these are women (Kim, 1983).

Research among each minority elderly group has yielded conflicting results about the weakening of extended family relationships. Becerra (1983) notes that some studies of older Mexican Americans (Miranda, 1975; Bengtson and Burton, 1980) indicate a continuing strong commitment to extended family ties. Other researchers (Solis, 1975; Laurel, 1976) have found those ties eroding. But certain demographic trends indicate that minority elders are increasingly living outside extended families. For example, poverty in the total U.S. Hispanic population rose from 21.6 percent in 1978 to 28.2 percent in 1987. The average Hispanic family's income declined $1,600 during that period (Center on Budget and Policy Priorities, 1988). While the Hispanic family extends emotional support to its older members, it is becoming more and more unable to provide for their financial needs.

Public policy also discourages the poor elderly from living in extended family situations. The Social Security Administration reduces a Supplemental Security Income (SSI) recipient's benefits by one-third when he or she lives in another's household for a full month and receives in-kind maintenance and support. This provision may cause some low-income elderly to be unnecessarily or prematurely institutionalized. It discourages families from helping low-income parents and grandparents who may receive SSI.

Health status also determines living arrangements. Poverty and a strenuous work history mean that most older Hispanics experience poorer health at an earlier age than do their Anglo counterparts (Dowd and Bengtson, 1978). The same holds true for other minority aged. The 1989 Commonwealth Fund survey revealed that 54 percent of elderly Hispanics are in fair or poor health, compared with 35 percent of all older persons. A higher percentage of older Hispanics is functionally impaired and has problems with basic self-care activities and tasks of daily living (like money management and meal preparation). In fact, compared to all older Americans, more than twice as many Hispanic elderly report problems with at least one task of daily living.

How do these ill elderly care for themselves? We have seen that most minority aged live outside extended families. The astronomical cost of alternative housing and nursing home care puts those options beyond the reach of all but a few.

Furthermore, the concept of the rest home—the *asilo*—has always been considered by Hispanics to be the choice of last resort, where one goes to die. Homecare programs are often unknown to minority aged, and prohibitively expensive. Thus many ill elderly are left struggling to survive in their homes alone, or with minimal support. Caring for a rising number of minority elderly in poor health will become an increasingly urgent public policy issue in this decade and beyond.

Fewer Hispanic elderly live in houses (68 percent) and more reside in apartments (29 percent) than is common among the total aged population, where the comparable figures are 77 percent and 16 percent, respectively (Commonwealth Fund Commission on Elderly People Living Alone, 1989). The difference can be attributed partly to the fact that Cuban American and Puerto Rican elderly are concentrated in urban areas where single-family housing is less prevalent. This fact illustrates another feature of minority elderly's living arrangements: urbanization. Eighty-nine percent of Hispanic elderly reside in metropolitan areas, as do 80 percent of older blacks (Public Health Service, 1990).

This demographic overview yields the following profile of a typical minority older person's living arrangements: an urban renter, usually a woman, living alone or with spouse only, struggling to make ends meet in a deteriorating dwelling. What options does she have for improved living arrangements?

Keep in mind that minority elders' acceptance of various options depends not only on factors like structural adequacy and affordability, but also personal and environmental characteristics that determine housing satisfaction (Struyk and Soldo, 1980). The physical features of the larger neighborhood; availability of public services; access to shopping, medical facilities, and social services; and the nearness and quality of interaction with their social networks are key elements of older persons' comfort with their living arrangement and social environment (Leven et al., 1975; Lawton, 1977). So are a sense of security and freedom from fear of crime. Desire to live in an age-specific residence (such as an apartment building for seniors) or an age-integrated environment is another determinant of housing satisfaction. Little research has been done on minority elderly's preferences in this regard.

For low-income elderly, federally assisted senior housing has been an important option. But drastic cuts in federal funds call into question its feasibility for all but a small percentage of the fast-growing minority older group. The Department of Housing and Urban Development's Section 202 program, which provides loans for apartment construction and rehabilitation for the elderly and handicapped, funded just 5,110 units in fiscal year 1990 at $283 million—a decrease from $327.1 million for 6,710 units in FY 1989. Minority sponsors received less than 17 percent of the FY 1990 funds. Only 25 percent of all Section 202 applicant organizations received loans that year. One positive development in the Section 202 program: New housing includes supportive services such as meals, housekeeping, health, and other services.

Federal preference rules have opened up more subsidized housing in private housing developments for people living in substandard dwellings, those paying over 50 percent of their income for housing, the homeless, and involuntarily displaced persons (*Housing the Elderly Report*, 1990). But older persons qualifying for such preferences encounter resistance from many housing directors, who state that they are "less educated, less cooperative, less socialized, have more personal problems, and are more illiterate" than other residents (*Housing the Elderly Report,* 1990).

Home rehabilitation programs—government-funded or unsubsidized—are a crucial option for older minority homeowners. Even minor home-repair programs can be the deciding factor in whether a minority elder can remain in an aging, but still desired, home. As direct government funds for these programs shrink, state housing authorities and local redevelopment agencies can initiate creative ways to finance them—for example, tax incentives to for-profit developers to undertake housing rehabilitation programs for the poor, or creation of linkage fees for affordable housing from commercial developers.

Some trends in unsubsidized retirement housing are largely untried among minority elderly. Home sharing, shared equity, housing cooperatives, reverse annuity mortgages for older homeowners, and similar innovative alternatives for helping older persons remain in their homes, have been tested mostly among the majority older population. And most of these approaches are not for poor older persons.

Subsidized housing is the primary answer to the low-income elderly's need for an affordable dwelling. When subsidies are available, then the issues of cultural sensitivity and architectural design become important. But to discuss the importance of creating unique housing models for poor older persons is ludicrous unless there are proper governmental incentives for subsidies to develop and construct this housing. Once the housing is obtainable, then innovation can be addressed.

If innovative housing alternatives remain untried among minority elderly, then the disparity between their living arrangements and those of the dominant older population can only become more pronounced. This would mean increasing isolation and persistent poverty for minority elders.

RECOMMENDATIONS

Here are some recommendations to achieve better living arrangements and social environment for older minority persons in the future:

1. On the public policy level, those aspects of government programs that hinder workable housing solutions for poor elderly should be eliminated. For example, Congress should repeal the current one-third reduction in the basic SSI benefit when aged, blind, or disabled SSI recipients live in another's household for a full month and receive

in-kind maintenance and support. Periodic, gradual decreases in the benefit reduction, rather than a one-time complete repeal, could make this $400–$600 million proposal fiscally feasible. Additionally, funds for HUD's Section 202 elderly and handicapped housing loan program should be boosted significantly. So should federal, state, and local funding for home rehabilitation and repair programs, and programs that assist the poor in paying utility bills. There should be more flexible age criteria in public housing to account for the fact that minority elderly age sooner than the dominant older group.

2. Barriers to affordable senior housing should be abolished. Creative rental rate subsidies for poor elderly, placing more subsidized housing in minority neighborhoods close to services desired by minority elders (e.g., churches), better marketing of affordable housing to minority aged, special incentives to minority housing developers (and to nonminority developers) to construct or rehabilitate housing for poor elderly, better enforcement of affirmative action requirements, and expanding the availability of low-income housing tax credits—all of these are ways to make more affordable, better quality housing available to ethnic minority older persons.

It is worth noting that in California in 1990, only 91 of 180 applicants for low-income housing tax credits received them. As a result fewer low-income housing units will be developed. Tax credit applicants (nonprofit housing developers) receive extra points if they build or rehabilitate affordable housing for large families and the homeless, but not for senior housing. That policy should be changed to include housing for the elderly.

3. Innovative housing alternatives should be tailored to ethnic minority elders' preferences, then tested with this group. Reverse mortgages and home equity conversion for homeowners, home sharing, housing cooperatives, and other concepts discussed previously can be tried with minority older persons. A crucial part of this process is educating lenders about the value of making creative financing available to the minority elderly.

REFERENCES

Becerra, Rosina M., 1983. "The Mexican-American: Aging in a Changing Culture." In R. L. McNeely and J. L. Colen, eds., *Aging in Minority Groups*. Beverly Hills, Calif.: Sage.

Bengtson, V. L. and Burton, L., 1980. "Familism, Ethnicity and Support Systems: Patterns of Contrast and Consequence." Paper presented at annual meeting of the Western Gerontological Society, San Diego, Calif.

Bureau of the Census, 1983. *Annual Housing Survey: 1983.* Current Housing Reports, Series H-150-83. Washington, D.C.: U.S. Department of Commerce and Office of Policy Development and Research, U.S. Department of Housing and Urban Development.

Bureau of the Census, 1989. *Current Population Reports: Money Income and Poverty Status of Families and Persons in the United States: 1988.* (Advance Data from the March 1989 Current Population Survey.) Washington D.C.: U.S. Department of Commerce.

Center on Budget and Policy Priorities, 1988. *Shortchanged: Recent Developments in Hispanic Poverty, Income and Employment.* Washington, D.C.

Commonwealth Fund Commission on Elderly People Living Alone, 1989. *Poverty and Poor Health Among Elderly Hispanic Americans.* Baltimore, Md.

Dowd, J. J. and Bengtson, V., 1978. "Aging in Minority Populations: An Examination of the Double Jeopardy Hypothesis." *Journal of Gerontology* 33(3): 427–36.

Herbert, A., 1983. "Enhancing Housing Opportunities for the Black Elderly." In R. L. McNeely and J. Cohen, eds., *Aging in Minority Groups.* Beverly Hills, Calif.: Sage.

CD Publications. *Housing the Elderly Report* 89(1):1. Silverspring, Md.

CD Publications. *Housing the Elderly Report* 90(7): 1-3. Silverspring, Md.

Johnson, R., 1978. "Barriers to Adequate Housing for Elderly Blacks." *Aging*: 33-39.

Kim, Paul K. H., 1983. "Demography of the Asian-Pacific Elderly: Selected Problems and Implications." In R. L. McNeeley and J. L. Colen, eds., *Aging in Minority Groups.* Beverly Hills, Calif.: Sage.

Lacayo, Camela G., 1980. *A National Study to Assess the Service Needs of the Hispanic Elderly: Final Report.* Los Angeles: Asociación Nacional Pro Personas Mayores.

Laurel, N., 1976. "An Intergenerational Comparison of Attitudes Toward the Support of Aged Parents: A Study of Mexican Americans in Two South Texas Communities." Ph.D. dissertation, University of Southern California, Los Angeles.

Lawton, M. P., 1977. "The Impact of the Environment on Aging and Behavior." In J. Birren and E. W. Schaie, eds., *Handbook of the Psychology of Aging.* New York: Van Nostrand.

Leven, C. et al., 1975. *Neighborhood Change: Lessons in the Dynamics of Urban Decay.* New York: Praeger.

Martinez, Charles F., 1979. "Policy and Research Strategies Pertinent to the Housing Needs of Minority Aged: An Example of Neglect, Inequity, and Cultural Insensitivity." In E. Percil Stanford, ed., *Minority Aging Research: Old Issues–New Approaches.* San Diego, Calif.: Campanile Press.

Miranda, M., 1975. "Latin American Culture and American Society: Contrasts." In A. Hernandez and J. Mendoza, eds., *National Conference on the Spanish-Speaking Elderly.* Kansas City, Kans.: National Chicano Social Planning Council

National Institute on Aging, 1980. "Minorities and How They Grow Old." *Age Page.* Washington, D.C.: U.S. Department of Health and Human Services.

Office of Policy Development and Research, 1978. *How Well Are We Housed?: 1. Hispanics.* HUD-PDR-333. Washington, D.C.: U.S. Department of Health and Human Services.

Public Health Service, 1990. *Minority Aging: Essential Curricula Content for Selected Health and Allied Health Professions.* HRS-P-DV 90–4. Washington, D.C.: U.S. Department of Health and Human Services.

Rosen, Catherine E., 1978. "A Comparison of Black and White Rural Elderly." *Black Aging* 3(3):60–65.

Solis, F., 1975. "Cultural Factors in Programming of Services for Spanish-Speaking Elderly." In A. Hernandez and J. Mendoza, eds., *National Conference on the Spanish-Speaking Elderly.* Kansas City, Kans.: National Chicaano Social Planning Council.

Solomon, Barbara., 1978. "The Black Aged: A Status Report." In *Policy Issues Concerning the Minority Elderly: Final Report.* Human Resources Corporation.

Struyk, R. J. and Soldo, B. J., 1980. *Improving the Elderly's Housing.* Cambridge, Mass.: Ballinger.

U.S. Department of Housing and Urban Development, 1991. "Section 8 Housing Assistance Payments Program; Fair Market Rents for New Construction and Substantial Rehabilitation for All Market Areas." *Federal Register* 56(70):18887–943.

Chapter 12

Politics, Diversity, and Minority Aging

Edgar E. Rivas and Fernando M. Torres-Gil

Older persons in the United States are a formidable political force, whether measured by registration and voting rates, proliferation of old-age organizations, or presence of silver-haired legislatures. But what about elderly members of minority populations? What role do Hispanics, African Americans, Asians and Pacific Islanders, and Native Americans play in the politics of aging? By most account, minority elders do not enjoy political visibility, are not a major component of the membership base making up the national aging organizations, and have limited electoral ability at the local and state level. Compared with mainstream lobbying organizations, the organizations that purport to represent minority elders are less able to lobby successfully and influence state and national policies for the elderly. What are the factors that explain this relative lack of political influence, and what is the potential for a politics of aging to develop among minority elders?

This chapter will discuss factors that affect the participation of ethnic and racial minority elders in the political process, underscoring the heterogeneity of the minority elder population and stressing that policies must reflect that complexity.

SOCIAL AND HISTORICAL FACTORS

The political status of minority elders is best understood by examining diversity, historical circumstances, and the social and economic status of minority elder populations. Elders from the African American, American Indian, Asian/Pacific Islander, and Hispanic communities make up the populations commonly referred to as "minority" elders. Recent data from the U.S. Bureau of the Census indicate that 29.5 percent of our nation's total population is 65 or over. Of the total 65-and-over population, 13 percent are elders of color (U.S. Bureau of the Census, 1991). Historically, minority populations have been relatively young groups. Today, persons over 65 years of age make up approximately 8 percent of the black population, 6 percent of Asian/Pacific Islanders, 5 percent of Hispanics, and 5 percent of Native Americans (Taeuber, 1989), while approximately 14 percent of the white population is 65 years of age and over.

The minority population is aging. The benefits of improved public health measures in this country and the increased longevity enjoyed by young immigrant groups mean that they, too, will see major increases in the proportion of persons considered senior citizens. Estimates are that by the year 2030, for example, about 18 percent of black Americans and 13 percent of Hispanics could be at least 65 years of age (Taeuber, 1989). Already, certain groups—Cuban and Japanese Americans—have higher than average life expectancy rates.

The historical circumstances of those populations play a role in the current political situation faced by minority elders. Early immigrants of Asian and Pacific Islander populations, moving to the United States in search of jobs, faced a host of anti-immigration legislation—including antimiscegenation laws—at the turn of the century. Filipino, Japanese, and Chinese populations faced continuing discrimination throughout this century, including the concentration camp experience of Japanese Americans. Hispanics have faced linguistic and cultural barriers throughout their life spans. Mexican Americans had to undergo deportations, Cuban Americans came to the United States as refugees, while Puerto Ricans have continuously been pulled between the mainland and the island of Puerto Rico. The racism faced by black Americans and Native Americans is well known.

What the historical background points out is that the experience of today's minority elders with the political process in this country and in their country of origin has not been altogether positive. A reluctance to participate and a fear of authority are not unusual for those who are first generation in this country. Added to that historical legacy is the socioeconomic situation of minority elders. By and large, all four groups have higher levels of poverty, lower levels of education, greater health problems, and a host of multiple jeopardies (e.g., language barriers, uncertain citizenship status) to contend with. Thus, to the extent that they want to vote and participate in old-age activities, their ability to do so is lessened by the need to manage the urgent priorities of shelter, health, and income.

Thus, it comes as no surprise that the mass-membership organizations such as the American Association of Retired Persons (AARP), the National Council of Senior Citizens (NCSC), and the National Committee to Preserve Social Security and Medicare do not have large numbers of minority elders. Minority groups must then depend on the goodwill of established aging organizations to represent their particular interests. Yet, evidence indicates that where the established groups must choose priorities, the needs of minority elders will be secondary.

An illustration of the power of older people is the repeal of the Medicare Catastrophic Coverage Act (MCCA) in 1989. Never mind that the MCCA contained improved Medicare benefits for all, those opposed to its beneficiary-only financing provisions wanted the law overturned completely. The poor who were to gain the most from the MCCA (through expanded benefits, subsidized prescription drugs) were not a part of the debate and, with a few significant exceptions, did not have the membership organizations representing their interests. Yet, the MCCA's repeal caused them to endure the loss of additional medical coverage that they could not purchase on their own. The MCCA issue demonstrates the lack of political clout exhibited by older individuals who are low income or members of minority groups.

AN EVOLVING ROLE

Minority elders have not always been a powerless, dependent group. Historically, in their countries of origin or in rural areas of the United States, they have enjoyed the benefits of leadership (political, religious, social) and political influence. In many traditional cultures, older people (usually the men) held power or status by virtue of their age and experience. For example, in American Indian cultures of North America the elders were consulted because of their wisdom. In Mesoamerican cultures, the cacique was the powerful leader until his death in old age or in battle. His power was absolute and unquestioned (Machado, 1982). The cacique's power was the basis for a gerontocracy, a society ruled by elder statesmen (Torres-Gil, 1988). Today's cohort of Hispanic, Asian, Native American, and black elders are likely to have been raised in those types of cultural settings and perhaps to have expected that they would attain some measure of leadership and influence based on their old age.

Over time, however, the role of minority elders has changed. The status of elders changes as immigrant populations, especially among the young and later cohorts, immerse themselves in U.S. society. Adherence to a civic culture, where merit rather than age is valued, and the effects of modern urban lifestyles and a "youthful" type of politics, where education, sophistication, and money define political leadership, erode the leadership of elders within their own minority communities. Those who were once considered leaders in their communities have been relegated to the status of dependence upon others for some of their needs.

In this country, those who are dependent upon social services must have effective political advocates and they must learn to maneuver through the social services system. Factors like the "youth culture" orientation from the early sixties, the coming of age of the minority baby boom generation, and the changes in families being experienced by minority communities have combined to erode the status of the respected elders in culturally diverse communities. No longer do younger minority individuals go to their elders for advice or assistance; all too often an elder is asked for assistance as a last resort. This does not mean that today's minority elders did not play a crucial role in the political life of their communities; many have—in the civil rights struggles, for example. As a rule, however, to be old no longer confers automatic political leverage among minorities.

CULTURAL CHANGES

The effects of assimilation and acculturation are important indicators in understanding the past and future potential of minority elders to be political players. Assimilation refers to the adoption of another culture ("mainstreaming") while acculturation is the ability to function effectively in another culture without giving up one's sense of ethnic identity.

Differences in assimilation and acculturation add to political diversity. Most ethnic groups will assimilate and acculturate by the third generation, thus becoming more like members of the dominant population. Some groups, such as Jewish and Cuban elders, function effectively in the economic and political life of U.S. society even though they maintain their language and ethnic/religious characteristics. Others may assimilate completely. In either event, we cannot assume that minority elders will always be politically disenfranchised because of historical circumstances, cultural factors, or social and economic status. Much of what we know today about minority elders is what we have learned from first-generation immigrants or minority elders who were reared in traditional rural societies, and thus we may unwittingly assume that minority elders do not have the potential to become politically active.

In time there will be greater numbers of minority elders who will be more active in the political process and may be better able to form political action groups representing their ethnic communities. At the same time, immigration will continue, and there will be greater variations between first-generation immigrant elders, on the periphery of the political process, and second- and third-generation elders actively engaged. The challenge for scholars, practitioners, and policy makers is to recognize that diversity and not assume that all minority elders are politically uninvolved.

POLITICS OF AGING

Today, however, there is little doubt that minority elders are politically disadvantaged in comparison with the political presence of older persons in general. The older population of this country is constantly flexing its political muscle. Protecting Medicare benefits, forestalling budget cutbacks, influencing political campaigns, utilizing the media, and organizing local chapters—all are hallmarks of effective interest-group politics. Nonminority elders are involved in electoral politics as voters, campaign workers, and elected officials; they influence policy decision-making at local, state, and national levels; they organize on behalf of their concerns, many of them (e.g., healthcare and environmental issues) intergenerational. For many, involvement in the political process is a continuation of a lifelong interest.

Older persons in general have made such gains in political strength over the past 25 years that, in the past five years, a backlash has resulted. The aged are accused of being too successful in promoting social policies and public benefits and too intent on protecting their own interests. The repeal of the MCCA was a milestone in causing many scholars and policy makers to question whether entitlements based solely on age were an appropriate strategy.

The irony of the generational equity debate is that it creates both bad and good news for minority elders. The political influence of older persons is under increasing scrutiny at the same time that minority elders and their advocates are attempting to achieve political visibility. To the extent that elders in general are criticized for being a narrow interest group, minority elders are at a further disadvantage because while they themselves have not been part of the "politics of age," they are being painted with the same broad brush. On the other hand, the reaction against the seeming success of the politics of age has caused the Congress and others to target their interest and focus toward the truly needy, and attention to the needs of poor, frail, isolated, and minority elders has resurfaced. Efforts to define the targeting provisions of the Older Americans Act to focus on minority and poor elders, expanded SSI (Supplemental Security Income) outreach, and concern about the problems of inner city elders may indicate shifting of limited resources to those who need them most.

That shift is a two-edged sword. It may benefit minority and poor elders in the short run, by targeting scarce resources based on income, assets, and physical disability. On the other hand, it may erode popular support for programs such as Social Security, the Older Americans Act, as well as means-tested programs, if the nonminority and more affluent elders feel they are not benefiting from those social policies. The loss of their political interest will ultimately affect all elders, including minorities and the poor, since those groups are not able to play the interest group politics game effectively.

The risk is that advocates for minority elders and the poor will in the long run weaken the entitlement nature of Social Security, the Older Americans Act, and Medicare by arguing for greater preferences to the most needy at the expense of others. As a policy and equity approach, such an argument may make sense. But in the crass world of political realities, it will serve to weaken the position of minority elders since they will not, at least for the foreseeable future, be able to marshal grass-roots support or employ lobbying or political techniques to work national and state politics as effectively as the American Association for Retired Persons, for example.

All told, older people's activism can be attributed to their increasing numbers and needs. The concerns of culturally diverse elders are sometimes overlooked or discounted in part because of their inability to participate in advocacy. While the resources necessary for strong advocacy have not been available to minority elders, the diversity present in minority elder communities has made it more difficult. A lack of consensus on the primary issues and goals has hindered cooperation. Meanwhile, the poor in all communities continue to be concerned with basic needs such as shelter, food, adequate income, and healthcare.

Minority advocates like the NAACP are being pressed by their older constituents to work on aging issues while confronting such problems as education and income in their daily struggles. Some organizations like the National Urban League and the National Council of La Raza have taken their members' mandate to heart and have become more involved in the field of aging services and advocacy.

Minority elected officials have a responsibility to make aging issues an agenda in their communities. Again because of the "youthful" nature of minority demographics, minority elected officials are more apt to focus their advocacy efforts on civil rights, education, and family issues. Their vision is short-sighted, however, when one considers the growth in the number and proportion of minority elders and the aging of their community's population.

Some members of Congress have kept vigil on the needs of minority communities as well as the needs of the aged. Augustus F. Hawkins, former chairman of the House Education and Labor Committee, and Edward R. Roybal, the present chairman of the House Select Committee on Aging, are two such members. The late senator and congressman Claude Pepper was recognized as a leader of the aging field while looking out for his Cuban American constituency. It is clear from the vast membership of the two special committees on aging in Congress that aging issues are important to elected officials, but it is not as clear that all those members of Congress are educated about or dedicated to meeting the needs of a culturally diverse older population.

ROLE OF AGING ORGANIZATIONS

Aging organizations as advocates for minority aging issues have a mixed record to date. Several national aging organizations have been criticized in the past for being self-serving in their advocacy efforts and neglecting the needs of at-risk elders. Groups like AARP and the National Council on Aging are perceived as primarily representing middle- and upper-income elders. The National Council of Senior Citizens predominantly represents retired union members, while the American Society on Aging represents practitioners in the field. There are over 25 organizations at the national level that represent some constituency dealing with aging issues. Although it is the primary responsibility of these organizations to represent the elderly constituency, many of them have not ardently considered the concerns or needs of older persons of color in their deliberations on policy and advocacy issues.

The lack of leadership on minority elder issues among the national aging organizations led to the formation of associations whose sole purpose was to advocate on behalf of older minority persons. These organizations were the Asociación Nacional Pro Personas Mayores, the National Caucus/Center on Black Aged, the National Hispanic Council on Aging, the National Indian Council on Aging, the National Pacific/Asian Resource Center on Aging, and a relative newcomer, the National Black Aging Network. While these groups represent their specific communities, they often collaborate on issues that affect low-income individuals across age and racial/ethnic lines. For instance, during past reauthorizations of the Older Americans Act, these groups have worked hard to improve language in the act stressing the need to target resources to "low income and minority older persons." They have also labored over efforts to bring the level of SSI payments up to the poverty guidelines. Efforts like these have enhanced the ability of these groups to speak on behalf of the elders in their communities and to command respect from the decision makers and policy makers in the mainstream aging field.

In response to criticisms from minority advocates, some of the national aging organizations are beginning to address these concerns by dedicating resources to pursuing minority aging agendas. The American Association of Retired Persons launched the Minority Affairs Initiative to promote advocacy on behalf of minority elders to assure AARP's responsiveness to the concerns of ethnic/racial older persons. Funding from the Administration on Aging provided support over the past two years for four mainstream national aging organizations (American Society on Aging, Gerontological Society of America, National Association of Area Agencies on Aging, and National Association of State Units on Aging), two national minority aging organizations (National Caucus/Center on Black Aged and National Indian Council on Aging), and one national Hispanic organization (National Council of La Raza) to educate their membership about the concerns of older ethnic minority people and to lend their voices to the national policy debates on these issues.

A few mainstream organizations have effectively advocated for minority elders without external prompting. Since its inception in the seventies, the Gray Panthers has advocated for low-income and inter-generational issues. Likewise Families U.S.A., formerly the Villers Foundation, has worked on issues benefiting low-income populations (e.g., SSI and universal healthcare coverage). Other organizations involved with the aging services network—including the National Association of Area Agencies on Aging and the National Association of State Units on Aging—have addressed and been supportive of efforts on behalf of the concerns of ethnic minority elders because of the mandates of the Older Americans Act.

EMPOWERMENT AND ADVOCACY

Empowerment and advocacy in the minority elder communities are not simple matters. They are fraught with debate within the different communities. While acculturation and assimilation will lead to greater diversity and potentially greater empowerment, the poor and the most recent immigrant groups could be left behind with a greater need for advocacy.

As noted above, the role of older persons of color has changed over time so that they have become more dependent upon others for political advocacy in their behalf. While nonminority advocates for the culturally diverse older population exist, in general this population must rely on its "own" for active support in order to gain power for change.

How can ethnic and racial minority elders gain power and clout sufficient to influence the national policy agenda and ensure that their interests are considered as part of the "whole" debate? One paradigm to be considered is empowerment of the individual used concurrently with advocacy and community organizing.

Empowerment, broadly defined, is the sharing of knowledge, information, and skills with individuals so that they can help themselves and improve their lives. Critics of empowerment argue that its use as a tool for change is limited, suggesting that without very strong follow-up and support, the resources used to "empower" elders go to waste too easily and can be better used by providing services. They also argue that even those elders who are already personally empowered remain ignored. It is the lack of organizational and coalitional strength, as well as the presence of institutional racism, that limits access to power, these critics say.

A counterargument is that empowering people within a supportive environment will act not only to pass along knowledge and skills but also to build self-confidence in the empowered individual.

The actual appropriateness of using empowerment within ethnic minority communities remains debatable. Given the proper conditions for follow-up, empowerment is a very effective tool for a target population functioning as the vocal agent for change. If, however, it is not possible to provide support to empowered advocates, then such efforts could be perceived as setting up the advocates for eventual failure.

Another consideration is to reinforce in older people the belief that they have inherent leadership and advocacy skills born out of their life experiences. They not only possess the skills and self-confidence, but they also carry knowledge that is critical for decision-making power. It is essential to demonstrate to elders that while they may not use the professional jargon of gerontologists, their own knowledge and experience are far more valuable. While professionals talk about "budgets" and "objectives," elders know "not to spend what they don't have," and to "have something to strive for." Advocates are most effective when they are self-assured and comfortable with the subject matter they are addressing. Without those conditions, empowered advocacy will not succeed.

Community organizing is often referred to as another model to be considered for using elders as catalysts for change. The basic concept is that a community is helped to develop a powerful, democratically run organization with which to advance its own interests and values. This concept assumes, however, that the organizers or members of such broad-based coalitions have the time and the resources to commit to organizing these endeavors. In a community of older people of color who may be struggling with daily-living needs, the demands of community organizing may be sufficiently overwhelming to defeat the entire effort.

CONCLUSIONS

Given the diverse needs of elders from the African American, American Indian, Asian and Pacific Islander, and Hispanic communities, and given their lack of political clout, advocacy with them and in their behalf must continue until they can compete for their own interests and gain power similar to that held by the majority older population. However, a delicate balance is required. An increasingly diverse older population cannot always assume that each subgroup, whether distinguished by race, gender, or ethnic background, should have separate services. At some point, some level of "basic" services applicable to all segments of the population will be necessary. A common agenda among diverse subgroups must become part of the political strategies for emerging ethnic and minority elder groups.

At the same time, as the older population in this country grows and its diversity broadens, society must continue to develop policies addressing the special needs of minority elders. This effort will require the cooperation of many diverse groups involved with domestic aging policy, including those advocacy groups working for minority elders as well as mainstream aging organizations like AARP, the Gray Panthers, and the National Council of Senior Citizens. Policies that support universal healthcare, strengthen income security for all (SSI and retirement plans for working people), and stress the importance of education for all members of our society will reflect the constantly changing needs of our nation's diverse population. Coalition politics is a more salient tool for bringing together minority and nonminority organizations. Emerging alliances between minority groups and mainstream aging organizations, as well as children's advocacy and old-age groups, are positive signs. Ultimately, it is imperative that policymakers keep in mind that not all elders are poor and not all elders are white. They reflect the diversity that they and their families brought with them from other lands. '

Thus it is crucial that we as a nation not only plan for the needs of our citizens today but also for the future growth and aging of our population in the future.

REFERENCES

Machado, M., 1982. "The Mexican-American: A Problem in Cross-cultural Identity." In A. Kruzewski, R. Hough and J. Ornstein-Galicia, eds., *Politics and Society in the Southwest*. Boulder, Col.: Westview Press.

Taeuber, C., 1989. "Diversity: The Dramatic Reality." In S. Bass, E. Kutza and F. Torres-Gil, eds., *Diversity in Aging*. Glenview, Ill.: Scott, Foresman.

Torres-Gil, F. M., 1988. "Interest Group Politics: Empowerment of the Ancianos." In S. Applewhite, ed., *Hispanic Elderly in Transition*. Westport Conn.: Greenwood Press.

U.S. Bureau of the Census, 1991. "Data for 1990, from 1990 Census of Population," CPH–L–74, Modified Age and Race Count. Washington D.C.: Government Printing Office.

Chapter 13

Ethnicity, Crime, and Aging: Risk Factors and Adaptation

Wilbur H. Watson

This chapter develops an inquiry into the relationship between crime and aging, with special reference to ethnic minority elders. While it addresses the older person as victim of criminality, the essay also discusses the criminality of older persons. Included among the factors helping to account for victimization and criminality are socioeconomic class, ethnic identity, cultural background, social context of the offense, age of the offender, motivation, and the relationship between the victim and the offender.

AGE AND CRIME RATES

According to the U.S. Law Enforcement Assistance Administration (LEAA), there was an age-gradient in rates of victimization in 1973. A survey conducted in that year showed a decline in rates of victimization with increasing age of the victim (Cook and Cook, 1976). Although not specific to all forms of victimization, a recent study by Clayton et al. (1987) on elder homicide confirms this gradient. This study, however, adds an important qualifier. Among persons 55 years of age and older, homicide rates appeared to be increasing more rapidly since 1960 than among any other age segments (Clayton et al., 1987.) Older white men were the solitary exception: The homicide rate among them showed evidence of a decline during the same time period.

Very important to assessing the reliability of these reports on age-related rates of victimization is the confidence that we can have in the source of data. Wide-ranging discrepancies have been observed among reports of victimization (House Select Committee on Aging, 1977). In a study of 13 large cities carried out by the U.S. Department of Justice (1975), it was found that these cities had higher rates of criminal victimization of the aged than previously reported by the Federal Bureau of Investigation (FBI). The rates for larceny with physical assault were found to be higher for the minority elderly in the urban centers than was reported when analyses included rural areas and small towns. As such, the high frequency of fear of crime among the urban elderly may actually reflect objective criteria (Lebowitz, 1975). Further, the fact that the elderly watch television, listen to the radio, and read the newspaper far more than any other age group (Oyer and Oyer, 1976) may help to account for the widespread fear of crime and the self-imposed house arrest or self-confinement among them.

RISK FACTORS

Poverty and Ethnic Group Segregation

The incidence of poverty among African Americans and Hispanics has, for decades, been significantly higher than that for white Americans (Wilson, 1987). Partly as a consequence, African American and Hispanic older persons have had fewer residential options (Clayton et al., 1987). Living in low-income areas with large numbers of school dropouts, unemployed persons, and high crime rates increases the risk of victimization through disproportionate exposure of the elderly or their close proximity to persons who are highly likely to commit crimes (Wolfgang, 1958; House Select Committee on Aging, 1977, p. 18; McAdoo, 1979). Recent research by Clayton et al. (1987) suggests that black unmarried males, 15–24 years of age, should be added to this list of contextual risk factors.

Being in the Wrong Place at the Wrong Time

Older frail persons who go shopping, day or night (but especially at night), without an escort place themselves at risk of robbery and assault. Going out at dark in high-crime areas increases that risk (House Select Committee on Aging, 1977). By contrast, selective avoidance of these places of high risk can help improve the well-being of the elderly (Sampson, 1985).

Impaired Flight Responses

Self-defense or an attempt to escape from a putative assault or violent act, for example by leaving the scene or running from the perpetrator, is normal behavior among members of human groups (Silver and Wortman, 1980). With advancing age, however, diminished cognitive and motor abilities may impair the ability to flee from an assailant. For example, ambulatory impairment due to arthritis, partial paralysis, or late stages of a degenerative disease, such as Parkinson's or Alzheimer's, may obstruct flight under conditions in which a nonimpaired person could successfully fend off or escape from the assailant. To some extent, then, the incidence of criminal victimization of older persons may be accounted for by impairment of the flight response or by an act of omission, namely, the inability to escape.

Recent surveys show that with the increased infirmity often accompanying old age, many older persons in the United States limit or change their patterns of living in order to minimize their risks of victimization (House Select Committee on Aging, 1977, p. 18; Clayton et al., 1987). Some studies of fear of crime among the elderly show that this phenomenon, aside from actual victimization, often decisively affects their behavior in everyday life (Lebowitz, 1975; McAdoo, 1979). People over 70 years of age tend to be more fearful of victimization than any other age group (McAdoo, 1979).

Self-imposed house arrest, discussed below, represents one form of change in lifestyle that has been observed as a response to fear of crime among the elderly (McAdoo, 1979). While many persons are subject to the risk of multiple impairment in activities of daily living after age 65, older minorities in the United States are disproportionately at risk because of high rates of protracted poverty, ghettoized living arrangements, and poor police protection. In addition, deficiencies in ability to conduct the activities of daily living further contribute to impairment of their options for avoiding risks of victimization (House Select Committee on Aging, 1977).

SELF-IMPOSED HOUSE ARREST

It is generally agreed that mankind has the ability to adapt to a wide variety of adverse environmental conditions. Self-confinement is a coping mechanism often used by persons, including the elderly, in high-crime urban environments. In some respects, self-confinement has merit, as noted in congressional hearings of the House Select Committee on Aging, (1977, pp. 17–18): "Large numbers of the elderly, particularly the urban elderly, have restricted their trips in the community to those that are essential. They have virtually eliminated outside travel after sunset, and they avoid specific areas in the community."

As consequences of these adjustments, many older persons have reduced their chances of becoming victims of crime and may be at lesser risk of victimization in certain places and times of day than members of other population groups who show less fear of crime. Comparisons of data on victimization rates among persons over 65 versus younger age groups may underestimate the victimization rates of older people, or conversely, overestimate the rates for younger age groups if these studies do not control for the spacial and temporal circumstances of risk.

These questions about the juxtapositions of selected spatial and temporal situations as contexts in which risks of victimization may be increased (or decreased), and the elderly's selective avoidances of these junctures, are issues in need of closer study. Based upon the source and the kind of data used—for example, police versus eye witnesses—rates of victimization may vary widely, from claims of no problem of note to evidence of significant victimization in the same community. Underreporting is clearly a major problem in the use of police data and FBI reports, which are based primarily on police records.

The older person's subjective sense of risk and subsequent act of self-confinement, to some extent, help to break the chain of events that would otherwise set the stage for his or her risk of victimization outside the protective confines of home. Unfortunately, however, self-confinement is not fool-proof. It does little to prevent the offender from invading the dwelling unit or to constrain a family member or caregiver from becoming an offender (Clayton et al., 1987). Elder abuse, which is inflicted most frequently behind closed doors of private homes by a member of the elder's family or a nonfamily caregiver, is a well-known example of this kind of victimization. For example, burglary and household larceny led the list of household crimes in 1975 (House Select Committee on Aging, 1977, pp. 4–8) and were also well represented among offenses in 1988 (U.S. Department of Justice, 1990).

CRIMINALITY OF OLDER PERSONS

Most of the literature in the area of crime and aging focuses on victimization of older persons, fear of crime, and adaptation. Little attention, however, is addressed to the criminality of older persons. Perhaps this is related to the small incidence of crime among older persons—an incidence that is overshadowed by the higher rates among young males. Other factors that may help to account for the lack of reporting and analyses of the criminality of older persons are what seem to be public and juridical sympathies for older perpetrators of crime (Pollak, 1941). Some research has also reported that there seems to be an expansion of society's tolerance for deviance with increasing age of the offender in the later years of life (Kratcoski, 1990).

The tendency to dismiss the criminality of older persons is not new. In the nineteenth century, people of several European countries felt and believed that older people had diminished criminal responsibility (Pollak, 1941). Nevertheless, criminality among older persons does exist, although the body of literature on the subject is small.

Among the documented criminal offenses, homicide and suicide have received the greatest attention. There is some literature on drug misuse and abuse, but it is primarily related to prescription medicines and over-the-counter drugs (Watson, 1982; Barrow, 1989). Because of space limitations, the discussion in this section will be limited to homicide and suicide.

In a study of 179 cases of nonjustifiable homicides committed by persons 60 and older, 72 percent of whom were African American, Kratcoski (1990) found that 81 percent of the homicides were the result of a quarrel. In 89 percent of the cases, the victim and assailant were known to each other; in 82 percent, the offenders were male; in 74 percent, the homicides occurred in a private home. Nine percent of the cases culminated in the offender committing suicide. In each of the latter cases, the perpetrator was the husband of the victim of homicide. The Kratcoski (1990) study indicated the presence of important conditional factors that may help to set the stage for criminal assault.

In addition to quarrels between victims and assailants, Kratcoski (1990) found that 44 percent of the homicide offenders had been under the influence of alcohol; in 40 percent of the cases, both the victim and the offender had been drinking; and of those who had been drinking at the time of the offense, 46 percent had a history of alcohol abuse. Histories of mental disorder of the assailant and the victim were also investigated, but the findings were less conclusive. These findings converge with Schuckit's (1977) earlier research on this subject.

According to Miller (1979), in his detailed study of geriatric suicide, people 60 years of age and older in 1975 accounted for 18 percent of the U.S. population, but 23 percent of all suicides. Contrary to their youthful counterparts, older persons threaten or attempt suicide much less often, but effectively complete the act with far greater frequency than do youth (Grollman, 1971; Miller, 1979). Among the reasons for these age-related differences in suicide are the facts that older persons are less likely than younger persons to communicate their intentions, thereby minimizing outside intervention. Second, older persons tend to use lethal weapons effectively (for example, a gunshot to the head), thereby increasing the likelihood that the act will be decisive.

Considering ethnic variations, the suicide rates for African Americans, Hispanics, and Native Americans are generally lower than the rates for white Americans (Miller, 1979; Busse and Pfeiffer, 1969; Lee and Rong, 1987). Although some of the literature shows significantly higher suicide rates for African Americans and Native Americans 15 to 29 years of age, only white males in the United States show increasing rates of suicide with advancing age (Miller, 1979).

TREATMENT OF OLDER OFFENDERS

The literature on societal reactions to older offenders suggests that the older perpetrator should be treated less punitively than his or her younger counterpart even when found guilty of the same offense. The rationale is that older persons who commit crimes may be misguided because of mental disorders or other maladies over which they have little or nor control. Another rationalization is that criminal acts committed by older persons are not (or are less likely to be) motivated by intentional malice for persons, property, or society at large (Kratcoski, 1990).

In spite of supportive public sentiments for older offenders, racial discrimination once again raises its ugly head when older offenders are brought before the bar of justice. For example, some research shows that African Americans and Hispanics in the United States receive longer prison sentences than do their white counterparts when convicted for the same offenses (Rand, 1983; *Justice Assistance News*, 1983). Other research shows that middle-aged and older offenders (40 years of age and older) who commit crimes for first time in late life tend to receive shorter prison sentences than do late life offenders with prior prison records (Bureau of Justice Statistics, 1983). Even under these circumstances, however, older whites, who tend to be more sophisticated in the uses of the "criminal justice systems" (or who get better lawyers), also tend to "plea bargain" and get shorter prison terms than do African Americans or Hispanics, whose cases are more likely to go to trial (*Justice Assistance News*, 1983).

REPORTING VICTIMIZATION

Class standing, minority group membership, distrust, and belief that law enforcement officers will do nothing; shame, especially in rape cases; fear of reprisal, especially by neighborhood perpetrators—all are among the factors associated with underreporting of criminal victimization by older persons and their significant others. According to some research, white middle- and upper-class elders are "wired into the system": They trust the police and believe that the police can offer some form of relief and assistance (House Select Committee on Aging, 1977, p. 19). By contrast, neither the minority middle class nor the minority poor elderly are wired in; they tend not to expect police assistance when in distress and often consider it a waste of time to report crimes.

CONCLUSIONS AND POLICY IMPLICATIONS

As shown in this essay, selected forms of criminal victimization of older persons, especially homicide, increase with age after 55 years. Robbery and purse snatching in public places are leading offenses against older minorities.

The literature also shows that many older persons have learned to adapt to their own frailty and risk of criminal victimization by refraining from going out at certain times of day when they may be at risk. This kind of adjustment is partly a response to fear of crime, but it helps to reduce the older person's vulnerability to certain kinds of offenses, such as assault and purse snatching. By ignoring this adaptive behavior and failing to control for time and place of offenses against the aged, many attempts at comparative studies of victimization of young and older persons may show significant errors in estimations of crimes against the elderly.

Future planning of housing for the elderly can contribute to prevention of risks of victimization by refraining from constructing homes for the elderly near low-income public housing projects. Young unemployed males, 15–24 years of age, are often represented in large numbers among the inhabitants of public housing projects and highly represented, as well, among perpetrators of crime against older persons.

This study also shows that the criminality of older persons is itself problematic. Older persons are disproportionately represented among victims of suicide. Both suicide and homicides committed by older persons tend to be private, occurring at home or among other familiar surroundings or people. As such, self-confinement is not necessarily fail safe as a buffer against victimization.

In regard to homicides committed by older persons, they tend to follow a quarrel between persons who are very familiar with each other and tend to occur in relatively private places. Murder-suicides are especially likely under conditions of previously long-term intimate relations spoiled by terminal illness of one or both partners. Less fatal forms of elder abuse, such as assault and battery and financial exploitation, may also occur under these conditions.

Finally, any thoroughgoing approach to remedying victimization of the elderly must also treat the problems of young males, 15–24 years of age, who are so frequently the perpetrators of crimes against older persons. Improvements in the health, life chances, and general living conditions among youth should help to reduce their disposition to prey upon their elderly, often functionally impaired and vulnerable, neighbors. Overall, many challenges remain for social research and advocates for prevention in the area of crime and aging.

REFERENCES

Barrow, G. M., 1989. *Aging, the Individual and Society.* New York: West Publishing.

Bureau of Justice Statistics, 1983. "Career Patterns in Crime." Rockville, Md.: National Criminal Justice Reference Service.

Busse, E. W. and Pfeiffer, E., 1969. *Behavior and Adaptation in Later Life.* Boston: Little, Brown.

Clayton, O., Baird, A. C. and Chandler-Clayton, A. C., 1987. "Structural Correlates of Elder Homicide: A Cross-sectional Study." In W. H. Watson, ed., *The Health of Older Blacks, Part II. Studies of Violence and Other Life Threatening Disorders.* Atlanta, Ga.: Center on Health and Aging, Atlanta University, pp. 5–30.

Cook, F. L. and Cook, T. D., 1976. "Evaluating the Rhetoric of Crisis:A Case Study of Criminal Victimization of the Elderly." *Social Service Review* 50(4): 632–46.

Grollman, E., 1971. *Suicide: Prevention, Intervention and Postvention.* Boston: Beacon Press.

House Select Committee on Aging, 1977. *In Search of Security: A National Perspective on Elderly Crime Victimization*. Washington, D.C.: Government Printing Office, Comm. Pub. No. 95-87.

Justice Assistance News, 1983. "Blacks, Hispanics Imprisoned Longer Than Whites."

Kratcoski, P. C., 1990. "Circumstances Surrounding Homicides by Older Offenders." *Criminal Justice and Behavior* 17 (4): 420–30.

Lee, E. S. and Rong, X., 1987. "Suicide: A Historical View." In W. Watson, ed., *The Health of Older Blacks, Part II. Studies of Violence and Other Life Threatening Disorders*. Atlanta, Ga.: Center on Health and Aging, Atlanta University, pp. 31–48.

Lebowitz, B. D., 1975. "Age and Fearfulness: Personal and Situational Factors." *Journal of Gerontology* 30:696–700.

McAdoo, J., 1979. "Well-Being and Fear of Crime Among the Black Elderly." In D. E. Gelfand and E. Kutzik, eds., *Ethnicity and Aging*. New York: Springer, pp. 227–90.

Miller, M., 1979. *Suicide After Sixty: The Final Alternative*. New York Springer.

Oyer, H. and Oyer, E., 1976. *Aging and Communication*. Baltimore, Md.: University Park Press.

Pollak, O., 1941. "The Criminality of Old Age." *Journal of Criminal Psychopathology* 3: 214–35.

Rand Corporation, 1983. *Black and Hispanic Imprisonment*. Santa Monica, Calif.

Sampson, R. J., 1985. "Neighborhood and Crime: The Structural Determinants of Personal Victimization." *Journal of Research on Crime and Delinquency* 22(February): 7-40.

Schuckit, M. A., 1977. "Geriatric Alcoholism and Drug Abuse." *Gerontologist* 17(2): 168–74.

Silver, R. L. and Wortman, C. B., 1980. "Coping With Undesirable Life Events." In J. Garber and M. E. P. Seligman, eds., *Human Helplessness:Theory and Applications*. New York:Academic Press, pp. 279–340.

U.S. Department of Justice, 1975. *Criminal Victimization Surveys in Thirteen American Cities*. Washington, D.C.: Government Printing Office.

U.S. Department of Justice, 1990. *Criminal Victimization in the United States, 1983*. Washington, D.C.:Office of Justice Programs.

Watson, W. H., 1982. *Aging and Social Behavior:An Introduction to Social Gerontology*. Monterey, Calif.:Wadsworth Health Sciences Division.

Wilson, W. J., 1987. *The Truly Disadvantaged*. Chicago:University of Chicago Press.

Wolfgang, M. E., 1958. *Patterns in Criminal Homicide*. New York:John Wiley and Sons.

Chapter 14

Caregiving among Racial and Ethnic Minority Elders: Family and Social Supports

Shirley A. Lockery

A rise in the life expectancy of racial and ethnic minority elderly—African Americans, American Indians, Asians and Pacific Islanders, and persons of Hispanic origins—has contributed to a rapid growth of these populations (Jackson, 1988). Coupled with the economic recessions of the seventies, eighties, and now the nineties, and subsequent budget cuts in human-service programs, this growth has serious repercussions on the future caregiving options for minority elders. Other changes in the society, for example, outgroup marriages, social mobility, and shifting (im)migration trends and patterns among racial and ethnic minority groups, contribute further to this uncertainty. Yet the consequences of these changes on the social support or caregiving networks of minority elderly have received little systematic attention.

The purpose of this chapter is to examine diversity in intergenerational family and social support patterns that affect caregiving of older African Americans, American Indians, Asian and Pacific Islanders, and persons of Hispanic origins. It should be noted, however, that much of the literature available to date has focused on African Americans and Hispanics, America's largest racial and ethnic minority populations.

Social support, a complex construct with many definitions and dimensions, is a dominant theme in the literature. Antonucci (1985) defines the multidimensional nature of social support "as interpersonal transactions involving key elements such as aid, affect, or affirmation." Social support also has a "buffering effect," which may minimize the likelihood of an undesirable experience (Kessler and McLeod, 1985).

The primary source of social support or caregiving, both instrumental and affective, for the elderly in this society continues to be the family (Brody, 1985; Stone et al., 1987). Affective support provides emotional assistance like love, companionship, and understanding. In contrast, instrumental support provides more concrete services like housekeeping, transportation, money, food, and gifts.

The informal support network of the racial and ethnic minority (family, friends, and neighbors), particularly the family, has been the fulcrum of their social integration. Later in life, this same support system becomes the primary source of caregiving for the older racial and ethnic minority adult. At times, the emphasis placed on the informal support systems of these groups has resulted in a tendency to idealize their availability (Cantor, 1979; Mutran, 1985; Rosenthal, 1986).

Research that challenges the assumed benefits and consequences of large and cohesive family support systems among racial and ethnic minority elders is beginning to emerge in the literature (Mindel et al., 1986; Mitchell and Register, 1984). Although racial and ethnic minority families have been known to contribute considerable amounts of emotional, informational, and tangible support to the elderly, their availability has fostered many erroneous assumptions. These assumptions bolster a long-standing belief that minorities take care of their own or that the availability of informal supports assures older racial and ethnic minorities of extensive social resources (Mindel and Wright, 1982; Mindel et al., 1986). Some families do provide extensive social support, but indications are that previous assumptions about racial and ethnic minority elders' social support systems are too simplistic. A high social density, a large family, or an informal support network is not an accurate indicator of social support. Moreover, existing family support systems that are assumed to relieve strain may in reality be the cause of strain (Robinson, 1983).

DIFFERENCES IN CAREGIVING—
CULTURE OR ECONOMICS?

Reasons for differences in family helping patterns between racial and ethnic minority elderly and white elderly are inconclusive. Some researchers link strong familial ties to race, ethnicity, or cultural values (Chatters et al., 1985, 1986; Taylor, 1986). Others (Mitchell and Register, 1984) suggest that family support is a result of socioeconomic factors. Perhaps, as suggested by Mutran (1985) in a study of inter-generational family support among blacks and whites, family helping behavior should be attributed both to cultural values and to socio-economic status.

In reality, what may initially appear to be a contradiction in the interpretation of the racial and ethnic minority elders' family support systems in the literature is actually a reflection of the diversity within and between the different groups. Many of these differences can be traced to such factors as socioeconomic status, the level of the elders' need, the availability of a spouse, children, and family members (including the number), the extent of acculturation, length of time in this country, and the circumstances under which the group or indi-viduals arrived in this country. Since these factors vary within and among each group, care must be taken to prevent the indiscriminate clustering of socioeconomic and racial and ethnic or cultural values.

AFRICAN AMERICAN SOCIAL SUPPORTS

To date, African American social support and caregiving patterns have been examined largely through cross-sectional survey research designs that compare elderly blacks with other racial or ethnic groups (Cantor, 1979; Johnson and Barer, 1990; Mitchell and Register, 1984; Mutran, 1985). As a result, the findings do not reflect the diversity within African American families' intergenerational relationships. This is further compounded by the fact that much of the research has focused on African American families from lower socioeconomic levels (Cantor, 1979; Lubben and Becerra, 1987; Weeks and Cuellar, 1981).

Research findings on the extended family and social support net-works of older blacks have been described elsewhere (Gibson, 1982; Mutran, 1985; Taylor and Chatters, 1986; Taylor et al., 1990). For example, African American families are known to be extremely involved in intergenerational support activities and are more likely to treat the older person with respect than is the general population (Mutran, 1985). Regardless of socioeconomic status, African American children and grandchildren tend to assist older family members (Mitchell and Register, 1984). Reciprocally, older African Americans were more likely to take younger family members (grandchildren, nieces, and nephews) into their homes (Mitchell and Register, 1984).

Again, the black elderly, more so than the white, received greater (albeit small) instrumental assistance from their informal support network. The more common types of support received were transportation, help with banking, homemaker services, and administrative/legal services (Mindel et al., 1986).

Data from the National Survey of Black Americans (NSBA), the first national probability sample of African American adults (18 years of age and older), have shed light on within- group differences. For example, Taylor (1986) validated the importance of available children to compensate for the negative association between age and the receipt of social support from extended family members. The value of family, friends, and church members as sources of social support for African American elders was also substantiated. In fact, church members were found to provide more than the expected socioemotional support through instrumental, including some financial, assistance (Taylor and Chatters, 1986).

AMERICAN INDIAN SOCIAL SUPPORTS

While the reality of significant tribal difference can and should not be overlooked, American Indian cultures have traditionally venerated the value of the extended family. Their elderly have historically been respected for their wisdom, experience, and knowledge of tribal history and customs. Therefore, many elders, regardless of tribe, assumed significant roles as teachers and caretakers of the young. Thus, elders on reservations tend to rely primarily on some form of extended family for caregiving. Those living away from the reservation, however, are forced to try to augment their supports through formal resources (National Indian Council on Aging, 1981; Shomaker, 1990).

Caregiving relationships among American Indian elders in the Southwest were demonstrated by their greater involvement in childcare than that of whites or Hispanics 60 years of age and over (Harris et al., 1989). Shomaker's (1990) study of intergenerational relationships among Navajo women on the reservation substantiated reciprocal caregiving patterns among three generations (grandmother-daughter-grandchild). Basically, Navajo grandmothers were found to invest in positive relationships with their daughters and grandchildren to ensure their own care in their later years (Shomaker, 1990).

ASIAN/PACIFIC ISLANDERS SOCIAL SUPPORTS

Cultural diversity within and between Asian American/Pacific Islanders populations is significant. However, many of these cultures are influenced by Confucian ideology, which accentuates the concept of "filial piety" and its focus on the children's moral obligation for the care and respect of family elders (Koh and Bell, 1987).

For some like the Chinese, restrictive immigration laws and immigration patterns weakened the traditional family support systems in the later years. That is, earlier immigration policies created a cadre of elderly Chinese men, most of whom are bachelors. Many of these men live in inner cities or "Chinatowns," without traditional familial supports in their later years. Thus bachelorhood, compounded by other environmental factors, forced the Chinese to become one of the first Asian groups to seek caregiving support outside the family (Weeks and Cuellar, 1981).

Unlike the Chinese, first-generation Japanese immigrants usually came to this country as family units (Weeks, 1984). The Japanese family was thus able to maintain some of the core values that enabled the elderly to be sustained "in nonstigmatized family roles" (Sokolovsky, 1990). Hence, adherence to the concept of filial piety by older Japanese facilitates their accepting dependence on children as caregivers without guilt or a loss of self-esteem (Osako, 1979).

The traditional support systems of newer waves of elderly immigrants are being challenged. For example, elderly Korean immigrants follow their children to this country in an attempt to maintain the traditional value system of the extended family (Kiefer et al., 1985). However, once here, many of the older immigrants find that they actually have fewer kinship supports than they anticipated. Many are unable to live in the homes of their children and may live in areas where Korean community support systems are not well developed. Consequently, for the first time, many of these elders must look beyond traditional family caregiving to formal organizations (Koh and Bell, 1987).

HISPANIC SOCIAL SUPPORTS

Despite the heterogeneity of the Hispanic population (Mexican Americans, Puerto Ricans, Cubans, Central and South Americans, and others), the Spanish influence on Hispanic subcultures contributes to similar although not identical familial characteristics. For example,

Hispanic families are known to have strong bonds with patterns of frequent interaction that are extremely important to their members. There is a deep sense of family obligation that often supersedes the needs or desires of individual family members. Traditionally, the elderly, who are held in high esteem, expect their family to assist them in their later years and also to treat them with respect (Cuellar, 1990; Delgado, 1982; Markides et al., 1986; Markides and Krause, 1985; Schur et al., 1987). However, the recognition of culturally diverse customs, values, and traditions within each of the Hispanic subpopulations is essential for identifying ethnic-specific characteristics or behavior (Schur et al., 1987).

The complexity of subgroup diversity in the use of extended-family caregiving assistance among Hispanics is accentuated by findings from several studies. In times of need, older Cuban Americans sought only the help of their children, not that of other family members (Escovar and Kurtines, 1983). Puerto Ricans, unlike Mexican Americans, Cubans, and other Hispanics, relied on themselves or friends more so than family members for assistance (Lacayo, 1980). Finally, a high level of reciprocity was found to exist in the helping patterns between Mexican American elders and their children (three generational families) (Markides and Krause, 1986).

The purpose of each of the above sections was to briefly highlight the issue of diversity in caregiving, family, and social supports of African Americans, American Indians, Asian/Pacific Islanders, and persons of Hispanic origins. Acknowledgment of racial and ethnic minority families' affinity for instrumental and affective support of the elderly should not be taken at face value. That is, generalizations cannot be made about caregiving patterns, since there are many differences across and within the groups discussed here. Further, existing patterns of caregiving among racial and ethnic minority extended families and the impact on the older population are being questioned.

Unanticipated intergenerational changes emerging in the literature suggest that (1) older blacks who do not live with their children see both their children and grandchildren less frequently than do whites (Mitchell and Register, 1984) and (2) an escalated association of older Mexican Americans with their children increases the elders' chances of depression (Markides and Krause, 1985, 1986). Also, demographic projections for increasing numbers of older African American and Hispanic women suggest that other changes can be anticipated. These women are more likely to be widowed, impoverished, and in poorer health than their white counterparts. Such conditions not only increase the risk of dependency, they also contribute to a deterioration of inter-generational family relationships and an increase in institutionaliza-tion (Markides, 1989). These changes accentuate the need for shifting attention from similarities between and within racial and ethnic minority groups to distinctions predicated on the needs within each of the groups (Mitchell and Register, 1984).

SUMMARY

Further study and research must address the issues surrounding caregiving and intergenerational exchanges within racial and ethnic minority families before any conclusive statements can be made. The literature cited earlier accentuates the virtues of "traditional" racial and ethnic minority extended families and their commitment to caring for the elderly. This is problematic, however, since traditional inter-generational caregiving roles are influenced by many factors. Differ-ences in the socialization process, level of acculturation, "generation" of family and individual family members, years of residence in the United States, number of children, and the degree of contact with other family members and friends all contribute to variations in intergenerational caregiving attitudes and expectations. Clearly, first-generation families tend to be more traditional, expecting their children to assume caregiving roles in the later years (Weeks and Cuellar, 1983). However, children of the second or third generation usually find it more benefi-cial to become acculturated to the dominant culture, creating different expectations and often role strain between the generations. Thus, to better guide caregiving policies and programs for the rapidly expand-ing racial and ethnic minority elderly, policy makers and service providers must recognize intragroup family diversity and their implica-tions for needs and resources. Every effort must be made to identify ways of working with and supporting informal caregiving systems that are often already in place. At the same time, care must be taken not to perpetuate the myth that racial and ethnic minorities take care of their own. Not only may their elderly need more caregiving services, they may also lack the primary support systems that many assume are there.

REFERENCE

Antonucci, T. C., 1985. "Personal Characteristics, Social Support and Social Behavior." In E. Shanas and R. H. Binstock, eds., *Handbook of Aging and the Social Sciences*, 2d ed. New York: Van Nostrand, p. 96.

Brody, E. H., 1985. "Parent Care as a Normative Family Stress." *Gerontologist* 25: 19–29.

Cantor, M. H., 1979. "The Informal Support System of New York's Inner City Elderly: Is Ethnicity a Factor?" In D. E. Gelfand and A. J. Kurtzik, eds., *Ethnicity and Aging: Theory, Research and Policy.* New York: Springer.

Chatters, L. M., Taylor, R. J. and Jackson, J. S., 1985. "Size and Composition of the Informal Helper Networks of Elderly Blacks." *Journal of Gerontology* 40: 605–14.

Chatters, L. M., Taylor, R. J. and Jackson, J. S., 1986. "Aged Blacks' Choices for an Informal Helper Network." *Journal of Gerontology* 41:94–100.

Cox, C. and Gelfand, D. E., 1987. "Familial Assistance, Exchange and Satisfaction Among Hispanic, Portuguese, and Vietnamese Ethnic Elderly." *Journal of Cross-Cultural Gerontology* 2:241–55.

Cuellar, J. B., 1990. *Aging and Health: Hispanic American Elders.* Stanford, Calif.: Stanford Geriatric Education Center.

Delgado, M., 1982. "Ethnic and Cultural Variations in the Care of the Aged Hispanic Elderly and Natural Support Systems: A Special Focus on Puerto Ricans." *Journal of Geriatric Psychiatry* 15:239–51.

Escovar, L. A. and Kurtines, W. M., 1983. "Psychosocial Predictors of Service Utilization Among Cuban-American Elders." *Journal of Community Psychology* 11:355–62.

Gibson, R. G., 1982. "Blacks at Middle and Late Life: Resources and Coping." *Annals of the American Academy of Political and Social Science* 464:79-90.

Harris, M. B., Begay, C. and Page, P., 1989. "Activities, Family Relationships and Feelings About Aging in a Multicultural Elderly Sample." *International Journal of Aging and Human Development* 29:103–17.

Jackson, J. S., 1988. "Growing Old in Black America: Research on Aging Black Populations." In J. S. Jackson, ed., *The Black Elderly: Research on Physical and Psychosocial Health.* New York: Springer.

Johnson, C. L. and Barer, B. M., 1990. "Families and Networks Among Older Inner-City Blacks." *Gerontologist* 30:726–33.

Kessler, R. C. and McLeod, J. D., 1985. "Sex Differences in Vulnerability to Undesirable Life Events." *American Sociological Review* 49:620–31.

Kiefer, C. W. et al., 1985. "Adjustment Problems of Korean-American Elderly." *Gerontologist* 25:477–82.

Koh, J. Y. and Bell, W. G., 1987. "Korean Elders in the United States: Intergenerational Relations and Living Arrangements." *The Gerontologist* 27:66–71.

Lacayo, C. G., 1980. *A National Study to Assess the Service Needs of the Hispanic Elderly—Final Report.* Los Angeles, Calif.: Asociación Nacional Pro Personas Mayores.

Lubben, J. E. and Becerra, R., 1987. "Social Support Among Black, Mexican, and Chinese Elderly." In D. Gelfand and C. M. Barresi, eds., *Ethnic Dimensions of Aging.* New York: Springer.

Markides, K. S., 1989. "Consequences of Gender Differentials in Life Expectancy for Black and Hispanic Americans." *International Journal of Aging and Human Development* 29:95–102.

Markides, K. S. and Krause, N., 1985. "Intergenerational Solidarity and Psychological Well-Being among Older Mexican-Americans: A Three Generations Study." *Journal of Gerontology* 40:390–92.

Markides, K. S. and Krause, N., 1986. "Older Mexican Americans: Family Relationships and Well-Being." *Generations* 10(4):31–34.

Markides, K. S., Boldt, J. S. and Ray, L. A., 1986. "Sources of Helping and Intergenerational Solidarity: A Three Generations Study of Mexican Americans." *Journal of Gerontology* 41:506–11.

Mindel, C. H. and Wright, R., 1982. "The Use of Social Services by Black and White Elderly: The Role of Social Support Systems." *Journal of Gerontological Social Work* 4:107–25.

Mindel, C. H., Wright, R. and Starrett, R. A., 1986. "Informal and Formal Health and Social Support Systems of Black and White Elderly: A Comparative Cost Approach." *Gerontologist* 26:279–85.

Mitchell, J. and Register, J. C., 1984. "An Exploration of Family Interaction with the Elderly by Race, Socioeconomic Status, and Residence." *Gerontologist* 24:48–54.

Mutran, E., 1985. "Intergenerational Family Support Among Blacks and Whites: Response to Culture or to Socioeconomic Differences." *Journal of Gerontology* 40: 382–89.

National Indian Council on Aging, 1981. *American Indian Elderly: A National Profile.* Albuquerque, N.M.: NICOA.

Osako, M. M., 1979. "Aging and Family Among Japanese Americans: The Role of Ethnic Tradition in the Adjustment to Old Age." *Gerontologist* 19:448–55.

Robinson, B. C., 1983. "Validation of a Caregiver Strain Index." *Journal of Gerontology* 38:344–48.

Rosenthal, C., 1986. "Family Supports in Later Life: Does Ethnicity Make a Difference?" *Gerontologist* 26:19–24.

Schur, C. L., Bernstein, A. B. and Berk, M. L., 1987. "The Importance of Distinguishing Hispanic Subpopulations in the Use of Medical Care." *Medical Care* 25: 627–41.

Shomaker, D., 1990. "Health Care, Cultural Expectations and Frail Elderly Navajo Grandmothers." *Journal of Cross-Cultural Gerontology* 5:21–34.

Sokolovsky, J., 1990. "Bringing Culture Back Home: Aging, Ethnicity, and Family Support." In J. Sokolovsky, ed., *The Cultural Context of Aging: Worldwide Perspectives.* New York: Bergin & Garvey, p. 209.

Stone, R., Cafferata, G. L. and Sangel, J., 1987. "Caregivers of the Frail Elderly: A National Profile." *Gerontologist* 27:616–26.

Taylor, R. J., 1986. "Receipt of Support from Family among Black Americans: Demographic and Familial Differences." *Journal of Marriage and the Family* 48: 67–77.

Taylor, R. J. and Chatters, L. M., 1986. "Patterns of Informal Support to Elderly Black Adults: Family, Friends, and Church Members." *Social Work* 31:432–38.

Taylor, R.J. et al., 1990. "Developments in Research on Black Families: A Decade Review." *Journal of Marriage and the Family* 52:993–1014.

Weeks, J., 1984. *Aging: Concepts and Social Issues*. Belmont, Calif.: Wadsworth.

Weeks, J. and Cuellar, J., 1981. "The Role of Family Members in the Helping Networks of Older People." *Gerontologist* 21:388–94.

Weeks, J. and Cuellar, J., 1983. "Isolation of Older Persons: The Influence of Immigration and Length of Residence." *Research on Aging* 5:369–88.

Chapter 15

Rural Minority Populations

Share DeCroix Bane

The United States is made up of diverse geographic, economic, and political regions. Such diversity applies even more to rural America, especially when we take into account the various ethnic and minority groups living there. However, there are constants that characterize rural elders when compared with their suburban counterparts. Older rural people, by almost all economic, health, and social indicators, are poorer and less healthy; they have poorer housing, fewer options in personal and public transportation, and significantly more limited access to health professionals and to community-based programs and services (Coward and Lee, 1985).

This list of deficiencies and inequities may be surprising for those unfamiliar with the very real circumstances of many rural elders. It is often argued that being old and living in rural America is a form of double jeopardy whereby the individual is put at risk by problems of advancing age and by circumstances of rural residence. Minority elders themselves have a lifetime of disadvantages such as high unemployment rates, lower educational attainment, limited access to healthcare, and poverty. If we combine the disadvantages of rural living and being a member of an ethnic minority group or Native American tribe, a case can be made for triple or even quadruple jeopardy.

SOCIODEMOGRAPHIC ATTRIBUTES

Still limited but growing research exists on rural elderly; much less, however, is available on rural minorities. There is not at present adequate information to distinguish rural/minority differences and rural/urban differences within minority groups.

The majority of all elderly blacks (58 percent) and "other races" (51 percent) live in our central cities (Coward and Lee, 1985). However, the remaining percentage of these populations live in rural areas rather than in our suburbs, which are predominantly white. Native American elderly are the *most* rural of the minorities, with nearly half living in rural areas, particularly in the Great Plains and the Southwest.

Minorities constitute a significant proportion of the overall population in some rural communities. Blacks constitute a large segment of the elderly in the rural South. Hispanic rural elders are in greater numbers in the Southwest and West. Other groups are often located in small rural enclaves—the Amish in Pennsylvania, Filipinos in California, Vietnamese in Texas and Louisiana, and Haitians in Florida (Coward and Dwyer, 1991).

HEALTH

Race, ethnicity, and culture are important factors for healthcare providers to consider, as minority status has been associated with poorer health and reduced health and human-service utilization. Black elders have a 55 percent higher rate of diabetes (Type II) than do white elders (Lieberman, 1988). Three-fifths of the black elderly diabetic population live in Southern states, where the highest proportion of rural elderly blacks reside (Parks, 1988). Other health concerns of black elderly are hypertension, their number-one health problem; cancer, particularly for black males; and musculoskeletal disorders, which are prevalent among older rural black men. Barrow and Smith (1982) report that Native American elderly were eight times more likely to die of tuberculosis (that proportion is now greatly reduced) and twice as likely to die of gastritis, cirrhosis of the liver, influenza, or pneumonia. Diabetes and arthritis are also prevalent among this population. Since many rural elderly Hispanics have farmworker backgrounds, they experience years of hard physical labor and exposure to farm-related accidents and agricultural chemicals. Recent research on health, however, has indicated that it is important to distinguish between farm and nonfarm elders, with the farm elder being in better health than his nonfarm counterpart (Coward and Dwyer, 1991).

LONGEVITY

Some studies indicate that Native Americans experience the same limitations in their activities of daily living at age 45 as do non-Indian people at age 65. The National Indian Council on Aging stated that among the 85 U.S. tribes participating in Title IV (nutrition) programs, 41 tribes define "older Indian" as age 60 and over; 35 tribes use age 55 and over; eight use age 50 and over; and one tribe uses 45 years and older (National Indian Council on Aging, 1981). The life expectancy of the Native American is shorter than that of all other U.S. races: 65 years for Native American, 73.3 for non-Indian (National Indian Council on Aging, 1981). With lower life expectancy, the average Native American barely lives long enough to reach the age of eligibility for most entitlement programs. A similar case can be made for the Hispanic elders, particularly those employed as migrant workers, who consider themselves aged at 54 (Lopez and Aguilera, 1991).

INCOME AND EMPLOYMENT

Ethnic minorities have been disadvantaged in employment, receiving lower wages and fewer work opportunities. This discrepancy is even greater for rural minorities. In 1987 the poverty rate for black elderly was 31.2 percent in the suburbs, 29.2 percent in central cities, and 46.5 percent in rural areas. Black elderly women living alone in nonmetro areas had a poverty rate of 79.9 percent. This disadvantage affects applications for Social Security and Supplemental Security Income (SSI). Often these elders have worked in settings where there has been no documentation, making it difficult for rural minorities to apply for Social Security. When applying for SSI, Native American elders often find that their claim has been disallowed because of inclusion of tribal dividends in individual income.

SERVICE UTILIZATION

In general, rural areas have fewer formal supportive services available to the elderly than do urban areas. Informal support for rural elders is no greater than that for their urban counterparts (Coward and Dwyer, 1991). Minorities, however, have maintained stronger extended family ties both in rural and urban settings. Research indicates that rural minority elders are provided more informal support than are whites, but younger minorities are leaving these rural areas at higher rates because of limitations in education and employment, so informal support may diminish. Kivett (1982) suggests that in a rural area, race is of less relative importance to the life satisfaction of older adults than health and other social and economic factors.

Studies have indicated that rural minority elderly are often unaware of what services are available. Getting information to Native American elderly may be difficult because over 80 percent of Native American elderly do not have telephones, and the majority do not receive newspapers or have television sets. Even when rural minority elderly are aware of services, it is difficult for them to understand how to access the system to receive these services, and they often encounter blatant discrimination by service providers.

Transportation is the number-one barrier for most rural minority elderly because they cannot afford vehicles, road conditions in rural areas are often poor, and subsidized transportation is very limited. This transportation problem relates to accessing healthcare. Parks's study (1988) of rural elderly blacks in Arkansas, Tennessee, and Mississippi found that 47 percent did not have a doctor in their community.

In general, the rural minorities are the victims of many factors: policies that impose geographic and minimum population requirements; inadequate efforts to enroll elders who may not be aware of or may not understand the programs or the eligibility requirements; English not being spoken or read by some rural minority elders; deliberate discrimination against minority elders; and finally, culturally insensitive programs.

Sensitivity to cultural differences on the part of service providers is needed, as is a commitment to eliminating access problems and cultural biases. Far too often programs are developed by service providers without the involvement of the targeted rural minority elders. Meal programs and health programs are two important areas that can exemplify the importance of participant involvement in the planning process. The cultural background of the targeted group affects dietary habits and health practices. Cultural and religious practices will also affect the types of healthcare practice that one will pursue, such as folk medicine or other nontraditional alternatives. Studies on caregivers have shown that there are cultural and ethnic differences in what types of services are used. In general, whites will use both information and support services, including Alzheimer support groups, with far greater frequency than will blacks and Hispanics (Caserta et al., 1987).

POLICY

The crisis surrounding the provision of services to the rural elderly has only recently been given attention. The increased closings of rural hospitals, and the retirement (or leaving their rural practice) of physicians, nurses, pharmacists, and other related healthcare professionals, have had an impact on all the elderly, but their direct effect on minority elderly has often been obscured. This crisis is beginning to be addressed at the individual state level with special grants to medical training programs to include not only rural problems in curriculum but also incentives for graduates to practice in rural areas. Maintaining the health professionals in the rural areas is still a problem. Some advocate that reimbursement levels for rural hospitals and rural healthcare professionals need to be at a higher level. The marked reduction of public transportation, trains and buses especially, has meant the increasing isolation of the rural elderly from the full range of services. New and multiagency transportation systems have not compensated for this loss. It has been noted that the fastest growth in the older population will be among those with the highest risk of having limited or no ability to drive. Currently, a large proportion of Title III of the Older Americans Act funding goes to transportation. The current transportation system suffers from the fragmentation of its funding policies. There is a need not only to increase funding but to target rural areas and to provide guidelines that take into account the unique problems of rural communities (Older Americans Report, 1991). There is considerable discussion about the need to target rural areas in national and state funding formulas.

ADDRESSING NEEDS OF RURAL
ETHNIC MINORITIES

In most instances, it will take special initiatives, such as targeted funding and ethnic minority advocates, to address the needs of the rural ethnic minority elderly.

It is important to have influential persons as advocates as well as ethnic minority representatives on staff, advisory boards, and in volunteer positions. In parts of rural America the minority young are leaving, depriving the minority community of its better educated and more politically active youth who could serve as advocates on behalf of the elderly.

It is vital that rural minority aging programs support the natural network available to the elder rather than create new programs that do not fit the orientation of the community. The historical past of the churches and the rural ministers must be taken into account, with the inclusion of these focal points in such activities as needs assessment, grant applications, and the coordination of existing programs at the local level. Through cooperation and coordination, members of the aging network can build on the unique historical collective experiences as well as the cultural values and symbols of rural minority Americans.

REFERENCES

Barrow, G. M. and Smith, P. A., 1982. "Aging, the Individual and Society." In *The Minority Aged,* 2d ed. St. Paul, Minn.: West Publishing.

Caserta, M. S. et al., 1987. "Caregivers to Dementia Patients: The Utilization of Community Services" *Gerontologist,* 27: 209–14.

Coward, R. T. and Lee, G. R., 1985. *The Elderly in Rural Society.* New York: Springer.

Coward, R. T. and Dwyer, J. W., 1991. *Health Programs and Services for Elders in Rural America.* Kansas City, Mo.: University of Missouri, National Resource Center for Rural Elderly.

Kivett, V. R., 1982. "The Importance of Race to the Life Situation of the Rural Elderly." *Black Scholar* 13(1):13-20.

Lieberman, L. S., 1988. "Diabetes and Obesity in Elderly Black Americans." In J. S. Jackson, ed., *The Black American Elderly: Research on Physical and Psychosocial Health.* New York: Springer.

Lopez, C. and Aguilera, E., 1991. *On the Sidelines: Hispanic Elderly and the Continuum of Care.* Washington, D.C.: National Council of La Raza.

National Indian Council on Aging, 1981. *American Indian Elderly: A National Profile by the National Indian Council on Aging.* Albuquerque, N.M.

Older Americans Report, 1991. "Witnesses Call for Transit Reforms to Help Elderly, Especially Rural." April 26, p. 164. Silver Spring, Md.: Business Publishers, Inc.

Parks, A. G., 1988. *Black Elderly in Rural America: A Comprehensive Study.* Bristol, Ind.: Wyndham Hall Press.

Chapter 16

Creating Culturally Relevant Ways of Thinking about Diversity and Aging: Theoretical Challenges for the Twenty-First Century

Linda M. Burton, Peggye Dilworth-Anderson and Vern L. Bengtson

The goal of this volume has been to highlight emerging issues concerning diversity and aging. As the chapters in this collection indicate, current and future generations of the elderly are part of a quiet revolution—a revolution of older individuals representing the broadest range of ethnic, racial, cultural, regional, religious, political, and socioeconomic diversity ever witnessed in American society. This diversity challenges us to evaluate the applicability of existing research, policy, and programs to emerging elderly populations (Markides and Mindel, 1987; Colen and McNeely, 1983). And what is more, it prods us to reassess the relevance of gerontological theories and perspectives to the lives of ethnically and racially diverse groups of aged individuals (Bengtson, 1979; Jackson, 1985; Padgett, 1990).

The challenge to assess and develop relevant theoretical perspectives for the study of diversity and aging is not new. In the past two decades, gerontological research that explores racial and ethnic diversity has often been criticized for being atheoretical (Jackson, 1991; Usui, 1989). Given the emerging trends in diversity and aging, however, the need for relevant theoretical perspectives has become critical. Relevant theoretical perspectives are needed now, more than ever, to guide and explain what promises to be a very complex knowledge base on diversity and aging.

Social scientists face numerous challenges in the development of relevant theoretical perspectives for the study of ethnically and racially diverse elderly populations (Jackson, 1991). The most notable challenge involves the social scientist's "ways of thinking," or what Kuhn (1970) refers to as "paradigms." Ways of thinking encompass the social scientist's value orientations, perceptions of the world, ideas about the group of people being studied, and theoretical allegiances (e.g., conflict versus exchange theories). Ways of thinking predetermine research questions, methodological procedures, the assessment of established "facts," the interpretation of facts, and the development of facts into general terms that serve as theoretical perspectives (Dilworth-Anderson et al., in press). The challenge facing social scientists in developing relevant theoretical perspectives for the study of diversity and aging is that theoretical formulations are not often grounded in culturally, racially, and ethnically sensitive ways of thinking. Culturally sensitive theories of diversity and aging would incorporate concepts that reflect the relevant contextual and developmental processes of the groups being studied.

The purpose of this chapter is to discuss "ways of thinking" as they affect the development of culturally, ethnically, and racially relevant theories in the field of gerontology. Two issues are addressed. First, we provide a brief discussion of how existing ways of thinking—namely, the focus on social inequality—have influenced the development of theoretical perspectives with respect to diversity and aging. Second, we suggest some additional approaches and ways of thinking that may enhance the development of culturally relevant theoretical perspectives.

SOCIAL INEQUALITY, DIVERSITY, AND AGING

Among a number of perspectives that have emerged in the field of gerontology, only two have attempted to directly address issues of diversity and aging—the double jeopardy hypothesis and the age-as-leveling "theory." The double jeopardy hypothesis refers to the additive negative effects of being a racial/ethnic minority and being old on indicators of quality of life such as health, life satisfaction, and adjustment. From this perspective, aged racial/ethnic minorities are thought to be "doubly disadvantaged" compared to their white counterparts. The age-as-leveling theory is also based on notions of differential experiences related to age and race. However, this perspective suggests that the problems of ethnic minority elderly may not be that distinct from those of white elderly. While differences among ethnic minority groups are observed and incontestable, it is also true that the aging individual, regardless of ethnic background, is subject to a variety of influences that cut across racial lines and may mediate differences in patterns of aging (Kent and Hirsch, 1969). Thus, this perspective suggests that age exerts a *leveling* influence on the ethnic differences found among diverse groups at younger ages.

Both perspectives are reflective of the existing political and social ways of thinking that prevailed during the time they were developed— the early 1970s, when scholars and political advocates were focusing on issues of social inequality, discrimination, and racism between racial and ethnic groups in American society. While these underlying ways of thinking served to generate research and draw attention to the disadvantages that elderly minorities experienced in American society, the field was not advanced in terms of developing theories that examined "unique and genuine" cultural, ethnic, and racial group differences in the lives of the elderly (Jackson, 1991). These ways of thinking did not foster in-depth exploration of culture-, ethnic-, and race-specific group differences, for two reasons.

First, because of the emphasis on social inequality, much of the research tended to focus on exploring between-group differences in structural variables, such as income and education. Very little intensive research focused on identifying the cultural meaning and dynamics of aging within specific ethnic minority groups.

Second, because no available viable knowledge base delineated concepts that were culturally relevant to ethnic minority elderly, concepts derived from research on white, middle-class elderly individuals were used in ethnically/ racially comparative studies. The most common conceptual theme examined concerned "positive adjustment to old age." Even though standard measures of adjustment were used to look at differences among diverse aged groups, researchers did not study the "meaning" of adjustment for black, Mexican American, Asian American, Puerto Rican, and Native American elderly.

Adjustment to aging, as it is referred to in mainstream literature, implies that by employing certain coping strategies an elderly individual has achieved a specific "balance" in life. Existing conceptualizations of adjustment connote adaptation, conformity, assimilation, compliance, and at some level a passive acceptance of change. We suggest that because these underlying meanings of adjustment were not fully explored—partly because of the focus on issues of social inequality in existing perspectives on diversity and aging—they must now be reevaluated in light of the growing importance of understanding diversity and aging. Ethnic minority elderly, for example, may have a tendency to perceive aging not as a series of adjustments, but rather as a process of survival.

Survival and adaptation imply different mind-sets. Survival connotes an ongoing struggle to maintain psychosocial balance without loss of identity or integrity and in fact may mean that an individual has developed strategies to keep from adjusting. A rich legacy supports this interpretation among ethnic minority elderly, particularly black Americans. Ethnographic researchers speak of strategies for survival rather than strategies for adjusting in old age (Blassingame, 1972; Wilson, 1983). Black music, whether it be in the form of a hymn like "How I Got Over" or a popular rhythm and blues tune like "Only the Strong Survive," highlights survival as the ethos of black American culture. The message of survival is inherent in older blacks' descriptions of how they manage to live "through it all" (Burton, 1990). It is preached from the pulpit and resounded in the training that black grandparents provide for their descendants (Jones, 1973).

We are suggesting here that frameworks that go beyond a focus on social inequality are needed to develop theories about culturally and racially diverse elderly groups. These frameworks would reflect the many different social definitions, conditions, norms, values, roles, and cultural explanations that facilitate understanding of how diverse groups of people experience aging; we would know about variation both *within* and *between* diverse groups of elderly people. This level of theorizing about diversity among the elderly will lead to addressing more relevant issues related to specific aging populations and will broaden our understanding of aging in general. It will also foster the design of culturally relevant interventions for the ethnic minority elderly.

CREATING CULTURALLY RELEVANT
WAYS OF THINKING

How one develops culturally relevant ways of thinking, or perceives the need to do so, depends on a number of significant factors. Chief among these, in relation to the study of diversity and aging, is one's ability to move beyond traditional discipline-bound research methods, data resources, and theories. We would suggest three ways that may be useful in developing theoretical perspectives relevant to diverse aging populations: (1) the use of grounded theory; (2) the use of resources in the humanities (art, music, dance, literature, and folklore) as a basis for understanding and interpreting important themes in the lives of ethnic/minority elderly; and (3) incorporating a life-course perspective (temporal context and interdependence among generations) in the study of ethnic/minority aged.

The Use of Grounded Theory

The predominant method for generating knowledge about ethnic minority elderly has been cross-sectional survey research (Jackson, 1991; Markides et al., 1990; Padgett, 1990). Although this research has been a rich source of descriptive data, it has not provided the conceptual foundation needed to develop culturally relevant theories of diversity and aging. As noted earlier, with the exception of such studies as the National Survey of Black Americans (Jackson, 1988), most survey research involving ethnic minority elderly examines the relationship between constructs derived from studies of white middle-class aged populations. In some cases, these constructs are not necessarily relevant to ethnic minority populations (Markides et al., 1990). Thus, we are proposing that in collaboration with survey research, grounded theorizing, a method that *generates* culturally relevant concepts, be used.

With grounded theorizing, theoretical concepts and constructs emerge from the data. This method of theory building, which was first introduced by Glaser and Strauss (1967) in the early 1960s, has been specifically used in qualitative research, allowing qualitative researchers to systematically identify and extract constructs and relationship among variables from the data (Strauss, 1987). The constructs and relationships among variables are thought to be culturally relevant because they emerge from the cultural agendas and meanings respondents assign to the phenomena being studied.

The grounded theory approach may be a particularly viable method for developing culturally relevant ways of thinking and theoretical perspectives for studying diverse aging populations. For example, we know very little about whether the traditional constructs explored in the field of gerontology are relevant to the rural elderly or aged immigrants. Using the grounded theory approach, one could determine whether traditional themes in aging emerge in these populations in addition to identifying themes that are culture-specific.

The Humanities as a Resource

Social scientists have an array of untapped resources available to them for developing culturally relevant theories of diversity and aging. The humanities, for example, can provide a vast amount of information about important themes in the lives of ethnic minority elderly (Dilworth-Anderson et al., in press). The culture and experiences of ethnic minority elderly have been expressed through art, music, dance, literature, and folktales.

The literary works of individuals such as Gunn-Allen, Gaines, and Angelou describe in vivid detail the life circumstances of ethnic minority elderly. For example, Paula Gunn-Allen (1989) writes in *Spider Woman's Granddaughters* of how an elderly Cherokee woman provides her people with a sense of courage. Grandmother Spider is considered the link between the past and the present. She also represents despair and hope for her people. In other words, Grandmother Spider provides the context for understanding the existence of the Native American people. Context, writes Gunn-Allen, is an important part of understanding the Native American existence. This context is both ritual and historical in nature as well as ancient and contemporary. Therefore, an understanding of the past of an aging Native American is as important as an understanding of his or her present life. Gunn-Allen's work, unlike some empirical research, provides the cultural context for understanding the roles older Native American women play in their families and communities. Her book and others offer a way to begin thinking about and identifying concepts to facilitate the study of particular aspects of aging among Native Americans.

In *Just Like a Tree,* Ernest Gaines (1968) provides an excellent account of how aged blacks are rooted in a kin system of care and support. The extended family described by Gaines offers an explanation of how both blood and fictive kin are significant components of the black elderly person's support system. This story also describes the resiliency and strength of elderly blacks, as suggested by its title. Although nontheoretical, but theoretically enlightening, this literary work also offers ways to reconceptualize what constitutes a family and the different boundaries some groups use to define family.

In her poem *Our Grandmothers,* Maya Angelou (1990) provides a strong treatise on the concept of survival in the lives of older black women. Other literary works, as well as music of blacks and other minorities, clearly pinpoint how and why "survival" and "overcoming" are significant cultural descriptors of how one "lives to be a ripe old age." As noted earlier, among many racially subjugated elders surviving—not adapting, coping, or adjusting—is a key aspect of "successful aging."

What we are suggesting here is that identifying and using culturally relevant concepts may mean going outside one's traditional value orientation and training in order to identify and interpret what is important in understanding people from diverse backgrounds. Unfortunately, discipline-bound attitudes and requisites often preclude viewing sources of information like literature, art, and music as appropriate means through which one creates and develops conceptual ways of thinking. Nonetheless, if new ways of thinking about diversity and aging are to be developed, what may be considered unconventional methods might be a valuable resource in developing culturally relevant theoretical perspectives.

The Life Course, Diversity, and Aging

Recently researchers have rediscovered the analytical themes of time, process, interdependence, and context as they relate to aging (Hagestad, 1988). These themes are currently represented in the life-course perspective (Bengtson and Allen, in press; Elder, 1985), which demonstrates promise as a conceptual framework for studying the lives of ethnic minority elderly, particularly as related to family development, for two reasons. First, the perspective is based on "interdisciplinary ways of thinking." It emerged from the cross-fertilization of the sociology of age, age stratification perspectives, demographic cohort analysis, and the study of personal biography in social psychology and history (Elder, 1978; Hagestad and Neugarten, 1985; Hareven, 1987). Second, the life-course perspective represents a dynamic approach to the study of aging individuals and families by focusing on the interlocking nature of individual trajectories within kinship networks in the context of temporal motion, culture, and social change. This perspective offers the flexibility to design conceptual frameworks and studies that address a variety of issues concerning ethnic minority elderly and families in culturally diverse contexts.

By using the life-course perspective as a theoretical foundation, Stack and Burton (1989) have recently developed the "kinscripts framework" for studying aging among ethnic minority multigeneration families. The kinscripts framework emerged from ethnographic studies of the lives of older blacks in extended families and comprised three culturally-defined family domains: "kin-work," "kin-time," and "kin-scription." Kin-work is the labor that families need to accomplish to survive over time. Kin-time refers to the family norms concerning temporal and sequential nature of such transitions as parenthood, marriage, and grandparenthood. Kin-scription is the active recruitment of family members to do kin-work. Elderly family members involved in Burton's and Stack's ethnographic research were actively involved in kin-work through providing childcare and economic support for relatives, in kin-time by articulating shared family norms for grandparent and caregiver roles, and in kin-scription by actively recruiting and training younger family members to do the work of kin.

A detailed explanation of the kinscripts framework can be found elsewhere (Stack and Burton, 1989); it is mentioned here to illustrate three points. First, culturally sensitive frameworks for studying aging in ethnic minority families can be derived from a life-course perspective. Second, when culturally relevant definitions of aging and the family are incorporated in a conceptual model, the constructs created are distinct from those used in the study of processes in elderly mainstream nuclear families. For example, black and Native American relational arrangements determine their family members. For these groups family is defined as including blood and nonblood kin who mutually share a perception of their inclusion in the family and interact accordingly. Members are usually represented by an extended system of interaction and support. Burton's and Stack's focus on aging extended families yielded concepts that underscore the breadth and depth of kinship dynamics existing in ethnic minority families and reflecting their definition of family. A third point, which cannot be gleaned from the brief presentation of kinscripts presented here, is that the framework is potentially an example of "reverse theorizing." Although the kinscripts concepts were derived from studies of older blacks in extended families, the authors argue that the concepts can be applied to the study of older individuals in mainstream families as well.

CULTURALLY RELEVANT THEORIES AND THE FUTURE

The purpose of this chapter has been to highlight issues of culturally relevant ways of thinking as they affect the development of theoretical perspectives on diversity and aging.

Ethnicity is increasingly recognized as an important dimension of social differentiation in modern pluralistic societies. The term *ethnic subcultures* is often used to describe groups distinct from the majority population not only in racial or national background but also in terms of a shared history and cultural values. The question addressed by the chapters in this book concern the extent to which there are ethnic or subcultural variations in patterns of aging.

It may appear obvious that groups differentiated by ethnicity or subcultural heritage have contrasting orientations toward age and aging. Certainly cross-societal research has demonstrated that definitions of old age—its rights and obligations, problems and opportunities—vary across cultures (Fry, 1990; Keith, 1990). But it also may be argued that old age, a universal human challenge, brings with it problems and perceptions that are similar regardless of variations in social context (Bengtson et al., 1977). The heterogeneity of today's aged population means that the various criteria of stratification differ markedly among those now aged. Can such differentiation be seen with particular clarity as one examines ethnic groups growing old within the same broader cultural setting? Or are problems of aging generally common across groups to the point that social policy, programs, and theory may adopt a more universalistic perspective?

Ethnic and subcultural variations within the population of aged Americans have become increasingly discussed within the past decade, particularly as advocates from minorities point to the plight of elderly members of their communities. Yet researchers have only begun to accumulate a body of scientific generalizations concerning ethnicity as a mediator in problems of aging. Practitioners and policy makers have only recently begun to formulate programs reflecting the service implications of ethnic contrasts among elderly Americans. Both research and policy are frequently criticized as being insensitive, and therefore ultimately irrelevant, to current realities of ethnic differentiation among the aged.

Several questions that are emerging from this debate will most likely have an important impact on the development of theoretical perspectives on diversity and aging.

1. What are the implications for gerontological theory when the "minority" (of ethnic/racial elders) becomes the "majority"? This change has, of course, already occurred in specific geographic locales. In the state of California, it will likely occur in the middle of the next century. One conclusion is that we can expect to see even greater diversity in the future among the aged population.

2. What are the implications of the changing "contract" between generations (Bengtson, in press)? It has been argued that we are moving into a new era in intergenerational relationships, one in which the needs of the elders will be considered too costly to be assumed by their offspring (Thomson, in press). Given the importance of kinship networks in racial and ethnic minorities, we should watch very carefully the development of these "generational equity" issues.

3. What are some of the benefits of ethnicity in old age? As Stanford (1990) has pointed out, we have tragically discounted the positive contributions of having a distinctive cultural background. Myerhoff and Simic (1978) make a similar point in recounting the ways in which ethnic identity can be a "buffer" in the stressful changes of aging. We need to document the advantages as well as the hurts, the pride as well as the difficulty, of minority aging.

4. What research questions may emerge concerning diversity and aging in the next 20 years? This is, of course, what each of the chapters in this book has attempted to address, each in terms of its own substantive emphasis. We would say that the two issues under which most of the specific research questions can be grouped are as follows: (a) How can we generalize the common experiences and problems of aging, while at the same time retaining appreciation for the diversity of aging? (b) How can we focus on the changes that occur with age and at the same time recognize continuities between past and future? If we can keep these issues in mind, we will be better prepared to understand and take advantage of the complex diversity of our aging population.

REFERENCES

Angelou, M., 1990. *I Shall Not Be Moved.* New York: Random House.

Bengtson, V. L., 1979. "Ethnicity and Aging: Problems and Issues in Current Social Science Inquiry." In D. E. Gelfand and A. J. Kutzik, eds., *Ethnicity and Aging.* New York: Springer.

Bengtson, V. L., in press. "The New Contract of Generations: Implications of Population Aging for Conflict or Solidarity." In V. L. Bengtson and W. A. Achenbaum, eds., *The New Contract Among Generations.* New York: DeGruyter.

Bengtson, V. L. and Allen, K. R., in press. "Life-Course Perspectives Applied to the Family." In P. G. Boss et al., eds., *Sourcebook of Family Theories and Methods: A Contextual Approach.* New York: Plenum.

Bengtson, V. L. et al., 1975. "Modernization, Modernity, and Perceptions of Aging: A Cross-Cultural Study." *Journal of Gerontology* 30(6): 688–95.

Blassingame, J. W., 1972. *The Slave Community.* New York: Oxford University Press.

Burton, L. M., 1990. "Black Grandparents Parenting Grandchildren in Drug-Addicted Families: Issues, Outcomes, and Social Service Needs." Paper presented at the annual meeting of the Gerontological Society of America, Boston, Mass.

Colen, J. N. and McNeely, R. L., 1983. "Minority Aging and Knowledge in the Social Professions." In R. L. McNeely and J. L. Colen, eds., *Aging in Minority Groups*. Beverly Hills, Calif: Sage.

Dilworth-Anderson, P., Boulin-Johnson, L. and Burton, L. M., in press. "Reframing Theories for Understanding Race, Ethnicity, and Families." In P. G. Boss et al., eds., *Sourcebook of Family Theories and Methods: A Contextual Approach*. New York: Plenum.

Elder, G. H., 1978. "Family History and the Life Course." In T. K. Hareven, ed., *Transitions: The Family and the Life Course in Historical Perspectives*. New York: Academic Press.

Elder, G. H., 1985. "Household, Kinship, and the Life Course: Perspectives on Black Families and Children." In M. Spencer, E. Brookins and W. Allen, eds., *Beginnings*. Hillsdale, N.J.: Lawrence Erlbaum & Associates.

Fry, C. L., 1990. "Theories of Age and Culture." In J. Birren and V. L. Bengtson, eds., *Emergent Theories of Aging*. New York: Springer.

Gaines, E. J., 1968. *Bloodline*. New York: Doubleday.

Glaser, B. and Strauss, A., 1967. *The Discovery of Grounded Theory*. Chicago: Aldine.

Gunn-Allen, P., 1989. *Spider Woman's Granddaughters*. New York: Fawcett Columbine.

Hagestad, G. O., 1988. "Demographic Change and the Life Course: Some Emerging Trends in the Family Realm." *Family Relations* 37: 405–10.

Hagestad, G. O. and Neugarten, B., 1985. "Age and the Life Course." In E. Shanas and R. Binstock, eds., *Handbook of Aging and the Social Sciences*, 2d ed. New York: Van Nostrand Reinhold.

Hareven, T. K., 1987. Historical Analysis of the Family. In M. Sussman and S. Steinmetz, eds., *Handbook of Marriage and the Family*. New York: Plenum.

Jackson, J. J., 1991. "The Current Status of Ethnogerontology and Its Complementary and Conflicting Social and Cultural Concerns for American Minority and Ethnic Elders." Paper presented at the annual meeting of the American Society on Aging, New Orleans, La.

Jackson, J. J., 1985. "Race, National Origin, Ethnicity, and Aging." In E. Shanas and R. Binstock, eds., *Handbook of Aging and the Social Sciences*, 2d ed. New York: Van Nostrand Reinhold.

Jackson, J. S., ed., 1988. *The Black American Elderly, Research on Physical and Psychosocial Health*. New York: Springer.

Jones, F. C., 1973. "The Lofty Role of Black Grandmothers." *Crises* 80: 19–21.

Kent, D. P. and Hirsch, C., 1969. "Differentials in Need and Problem Solving Techniques Among Low-Income Negro and White Elderly." Paper presented at the Eighth International Congress of Gerontology, Washington, D.C.

Kuhn, T. S., 1970. *The Structures of Scientific Revolutions*, 2d ed. Chicago: University of Chicago Press.

Markides, K., Liang, J. and Jackson, J., 1990. "Race, Ethnicity, and Aging." In R. H. Binstock and L. K. George, *Aging and the Social Sciences,* 3d ed. San Diego, Calif.: Academic Press.

Markides, K. S. and Mindel, C. H., 1987. *Aging and Ethnicity.* Beverly Hills, Calif.: Sage.

Myerhoff, B. G. and Simic, A., eds., 1978. *Life's Career—Aging: Cultural Variations on Growing Old.* Newbury Park, Calif.: Sage.

Padgett, D. K., 1990. "Consideration of the Ethnic Factor in Aging Research—The Time Has Never Been Better." *Gerontologist* 30(6): 723–24.

Stack, C. and Burton, L. M., 1989. "Family Scripts: Negotiations Between Individuals and Families." Paper presented at the International Symposium on Status Passage and Social Risk in the Life Course, University of Bremen, West Germany.

Stanford, E.P., 1990. "Diverse Black Aged." In Z. Harel, E. A. McKinney and M. Williams, eds., *Black Aged.* Newberry Park, Calif.: Sage.

Strauss, A. L., 1987. *Qualitative Analysis for Social Scientists.* Cambridge: Cambridge University Press.

Thomson, D., in press. "A Lifetime of Privilege? Aging and Generations at the Century's End." In V. L. Bengtson and W. A. Achenbaum, eds., *The New Contract Among Generations.* New York: DeGruyter.

Usui, W. M., 1989. "Challenges in the Development of Ethnogerontology." *Gerontologist* 29(4): 567–69.

Wilson, E. M., 1983. *Hope and Dignity.* Philadelphia: Temple University Press.

Best Practice

This section is devoted to practice. The first chapter, "Diversity Assessments," by John Capitman, Winnie Hernandez-Gallegos, and Donna Yee, points out how important it is for service provider organizations to assess and plan how they will take into consideration the racial, ethnic, and cultural background of the elders they serve. The authors discuss a number of issues on which organizations must focus in order to address the needs of minority elders. These include mission, governance and administration, personnel practices and staffing patterns, service offerings and caregiving approaches, targeting, and outreach and marketing approaches. There is a need for providers to accept the reality that America's aging population is becoming a more diverse group. By assessment and planning, diverse needs can be met.

The rest of this section highlights three examples of model-program and best-practice concepts that have been designed to serve the needs of the minority elderly.

The first, "A Multicultural Conference: The Experience of New Mexico's Aging Network," by Stephanie FallCreek and Rebecca Busta-mante, describes a model statewide conference that brings together multicultural groups of providers, consumers, and advocates to assist in developing and delivering education and training programs to the aging network. The conference, in its 12th year, provides a balance of diverse information for the provider and consumer, from beginning to advanced levels of the aging network, in a cost-effective way.

The second example, "Dana Is Joy," by Jeannette Takamura, describes a caregiving program in Hawaii in which volunteers assist the homebound and frail of several ethnic groups. The unique unifying aspect of this program is that it incorporates a Buddhist concept into its underlying philosophy. The idea of giving of oneself by volunteering time in a variety of ways is a major part of the Buddhist religion. Because of the diversity of the increasing older population, the growing need for caregivers of minority elders is becoming an important concern. We must become involved in the quality of life that the elderly experience.

The third example, "The Village of O'tabe," by Curtis Cook, is a discussion of a comprehensive Elder Focus campaign that strives to provide all the help and assistance needed by the elders in a small Indian community in Arizona. Those of us who are involved in the service delivery network for the minority elderly know there needs to be more planning to respond to all the services and care needed by the growing ethnic minority elderly population.

Joan Roberts

Chapter 17

Diversity Assessments in Aging Services

John A. Capitman, Winnie Hernandez-Gallegos, and Donna L. Yee

Images can say a lot about how we view various stages of life and how we view ourselves as a people. The typical image of a long-term-care user is a Caucasian woman with a silver bouffant hairdo and a relaxed smile, seated by her walker in the activity area of a residential program. But images such as this can be misleading, and in the case of services for our nation's chronic-care population, they are. Activity programs for homogeneous groups of frail but medically stable institutional residents represent only a fraction of the care for elders in this country.

Increasingly, practitioners and others are coming to recognize the diversity of this population. Service systems are now challenged to finance, provide, or monitor assistance with a range of activities—from household maintenance and personal care to skilled health-related treatment and transition and crisis intervention—in a growing array of community and institutional settings (Pendleton et al., 1990). Yet recognition and appreciation of diversity from the perspectives of race, ethnicity, and culture—a multicultural approach to human services— is only now attracting broad attention in care for the aged and disabled. Presented here are some practical ways to assess how well an organization is addressing diversity and multiculturalism.

DIVERSITY ASSESSMENT IN CONTEXT

Cultural diversity has long been a feature of American life, and this diversity is likely to become more prominent in the coming years. The aging of the general population in this country has been accompanied by even more rapid growth in the numbers of aged African Americans, Latinos, Asian Americans, and other persons of color. As the equal-rights generations approach a new century, a graying America will be anything but monochromatic, and its voice will be increasingly complex.

Increasing cultural diversity is anticipated throughout our society, and the projected work force in year 2000 and beyond will no longer be dominated by white men. This is particularly true in the case of health and social services for older people, where female workers are already the majority and persons of color are marginally more prevalent at every occupational level than they are in private industry (Peterson et al., 1991). Even so, in aging services as in industry, staff persons of color are underrepresented relative to their numbers in society. And numbers alone are an inadequate measure of an organization's orientation to diversity. The capacity to use a diverse work force as a strength and to offer useful services or products to all segments of the community must be examined as well (Foster et al., 1988).

In the context of a research and technical assistance program sponsored by the Administration on Aging, we have explored aging networks' responses to increasing cultural diversity among staff and clients in a number of states and communities (Capitman and Hernandez, 1990). One finding stands out most clearly. For organizations—and individuals—becoming multicultural refers to commitments and complex, ongoing processes rather than a distinct end-point. In this way, assessing how an organization is responding to racial and cultural diversity provides a model for other aspects of quality assurance. Rather than simply listing accomplishments and shortcomings, organizations and individuals can begin to identify opportunities for positive change. The potential beneficiaries are not only the regulators or staff and clients of color, but all staff and all clients.

Diversity assessment can, however, be threatening. As human-services professionals and practitioners, we have been taught that caring should be color- and culture-blind and that we as individuals are to blame if our organization falls below some abstract standard of the politically correct. In contrast, experience in diversity assessment suggests that each aging-services organization has come to its current status through the combined efforts of many individuals. Agencies are also shaped, at least in part, by a variety of external financing and program design features. Viewed in this light, it is more useful to focus attention on the potential benefits of a more multicultural approach to aging- services provision than on deciding whom to blame for which shortcomings (Batts, 1990).

FRAMEWORK FOR ASSESSMENT

Conceptually, diversity assessment for aging services is straightforward. Participants together address basic structures and operations of their organization and how they accommodate the increasing cultural diversity of aging-service consumers and staffs. Based on the answers, participants identify opportunity areas and possible approaches for implementing a more multicultural approach.

The actual practice of diversity assessment, however, is more complex. Considerable attention must be devoted to selection of participants, setting, and process for the assessment. Outlined here is one framework or model for diversity assessment. Implementation approaches follow.

Ideally, multicultural aging-service provider organizations reflect recognition of and respect for racial, ethnic, and cultural differences among elders and other consumers of eldercare services in their community. Such recognition and respect are reflected in the goals, procedures, and outcomes of the organization and network at every level (Batts, 1990; Bell et al., 1976; Scannel, 1989; Watson and Clayton, 1988, 1989) and can be seen in each of the following, as described below: mission, governance and administration, personnel practices and staffing patterns, service offerings and caregiving approaches, targeting, and outreach and marketing approaches. By comparing one's own organization to this perhaps ideallistic standard, potential areas for movement toward a more multicultural approach can be identified.

Mission

In general, multicultural aging-service providers have an explicit commitment to serve elders from all racial, ethnic, and cultural groups. This commitment goes beyond a mere statement that services will be provided regardless of individual background and includes a stated focus on reaching out to all population groups. In some cases, organizations have emerged in response to the needs and desires of a particular subpopulation or ethnic group, and so their mission includes a special concern for this constituency. Yet even these organizations may come to recognize that their unique approaches to care may have value for a broader cross-section of the community, and they can develop a commitment to reach out beyond their traditional clientele.

Governance and Administration

Providers of multicultural aging services include in their governance and administrative structure persons from each of the major racial and ethnic groups in their community. The providers affirmatively seek to achieve at least proportional representation of persons of color in the context of an ongoing commitment to excellence in the preparation and character of all governing board members, other volunteers, and employees. More important for these organizations than numerical goals are ongoing explicit efforts to empower all governing board members and administrative personnel to participate meaningfully in funding, personnel, program, and other policy decisions as well as in the role of spokespersons for the organization. Empowerment of board members and administrators may also take such forms as including persons of color among those who attend national or regional training events and scheduling explicit opportunities for board and staff to assess whether the organization is meeting its multicultural goals.

Personnel Practices and Staffing Patterns

The personnel practices of providers of multicultural aging services include the following: explicit outreach to communities of color in recruitment; conducting of preservice and continuing education in languages, locales, and formats that are accessible; inclusive management and supervision processes that respect the varying contributions and styles of culturally diverse staff; and recognition of differences among staff in needs for leave, holiday, work schedules, and other aspects of employee benefits through flexible plans. These organizations seek to achieve representation at all levels of all groups in numbers that are at least proportional to their numbers in the broader community. They also pay attention to retention and promotion rate differences among subgroups of employees because they recognize that each function of the agency or network is potentially enhanced through a diverse work force. Rather than worrying about numerical goals, they are affirmatively committed to inclusive staffing patterns as an advantage in increasingly competitive labor markets and changing consumer populations.

Service Offerings and Caregiving Approaches

Providers of multicultural aging services seek to make their services accessible, understandable, and useful to all segments of the community. They recognize that different subpopulations may prefer some services to others and attempt to ensure that desirable services for each subgroup are available. This approach may also include locating facilities within communities of color and seeing that transportation to and from these facilities is adequate. There is recognition that some services can be more useful when offered differently or at different times so that homogeneous as well as heterogeneous groups can use them. For assessment, care planning, coordination with other providers, and direct care, multicultural organizations use professional and paraprofessional staff who are attuned to cultural factors in any caregiver-consumer interaction. Staff are attentive to such matters as (1) cultural differences in both food preferences and meanings associated with food preparation and serving, and (2) racial differences in both personal care routines and the status attributed to nursing personnel, for example. Staff are trained to empower consumers by asking them what they wish to be called, how they want care delivered, and how they are feeling about the caregiving situation. By encouraging staff to focus on how racial or ethnic differences may matter in each interaction with care recipients, these organizations come to define quality of care as treating each client as the product of a unique and valid personal and cultural heritage.

Targeting

Multicultural organizations have an explicit commitment to understanding the relative prevalence of needs for the services offered by their agency within the various racial and ethnic cultural groups in their community. Racial/ethnic differences in the incidence of specific chronic diseases—but also in poverty levels; isolation due to social, linguistic, or geographic factors; availability of informal supports; and help-seeking—all produce important differences in the timing, sequence, and types of services needed by subgroups in a community. Providers of multicultural aging services have analyzed these patterns and have reasonable targeting goals: They recognize that some services should be used to a greater extent by elders of color in their community than would be indicated by demographics alone, while other services may be used less than community race/ethnicity distributions would suggest. These providers proactively work with other agencies to remove barriers to referral or use of their service by groups who have not used them traditionally, and the providers continue to build or maintain strong links with referral sources in the diverse racial and ethnic communities they serve.

Outreach and Marketing Approaches

Providers of multicultural aging services express their determination to serve all elders in their community through marketing and outreach efforts that are appreciative of differences in message and method. The potential benefits of a service may be understood differently by each group, and multicultural providers have spent the time to learn about these differences. Similarly, these providers have learned where elders of all groups who might benefit from their services turn for information. These providers use the media targeted to communities of color as well as mainstream outlets and are conscious of linguistic or other factors that may obscure their message to these communities. These providers also use less-traditional outreach efforts by enlisting appropriate leaders, clergy, and community workers in their methods for helping all elders know about service options.

APPLYING THE ASSESSMENT FRAMEWORK

The characteristics of a multicultural aging-services provider can be an important starting point in assessing how an agency or network is reacting to increasingly diverse consumers and workers. But applying this framework in a particular organization requires some careful thought about participants, setting, and process. Before considering any of these factors, there needs to be a clear indication of commitment from agency and network leaders to the process of providing multicultural human services. In the absence of such explicit leadership, all other efforts to encourage an honest and productive intergroup communication may appear hollow to those who feel least supported by the organization.

The goal in participant selection is to develop as broad a group as possible to represent the diversity of agency roles and racial/ethnic groups in the organization or network. It may be appropriate for agency leaders to appoint an inclusive planning group charged with identifying the most effective set of potential participants.

The selection of setting and process for a diversity assessment should be aimed at facilitating frank exchange of opinions while minimizing any potential negative consequences for those who express unpopular views. It may be desirable to engage the assistance of outside consultants with experience in diversity issues and the creation of safe environments for exchange across cultures and agency roles. Such a consultant or an internal facilitator should assist participants in agreeing to maintain confidentiality, grounding their contributions to the discussion in personal experience, and taking responsibility for themselves. Procedures need to be developed so that all viewpoints expressed are given equal weight. Any summary report should maintain confidentiality and acknowledge the contributions of participants.

NEXT STEPS

Diversity assessment is not an end in itself but rather an opportunity for all participants in an organization to examine their own and each other's experiences to determine whether differences among staff and elders are recognized and respected. Diversity assessment can be incorporated in broader quality assurance and strategic planning efforts by aging organizations. In either case, the programs we have conducted around the county suggest that there are two major potential outcomes for the organization. First, participants and others may learn that exchanging views and experiences around issues of race and ethnicity can occur in the context of ongoing professional relationships. As co-workers gain confidence in having these sometimes difficult conversations, they are often encouraged to develop stronger and more effective working relationships. Second, organizations often identify relatively straightforward areas for positive change that will allow the organization to meet the increasingly complex needs of elders in this country. What is more, organizational changes designed to benefit elders and staff of color often turn out to provide opportunities for all consumers and the organization as a whole. In the end, diversity assessments for aging-services providers can present an opportunity to improve our responsiveness and effectiveness in caring for the complex needs of all elders.

REFERENCES

Batts, V., 1990. "Overview of Strategies for Creating a Multicultural Work Force." *Consulting Psychology Bulletin* 42(1): 37–46.

Bell, D., Kasschau, H. and Zellman, G., 1976. *Delivering Services to Elderly Members of Minority Groups: A Critical Review of the Literature.* Santa Monica, Calif.: Rand Corporation.

Capitman, J. A. and Hernandez, W. M., 1990. *Emerging Issues in Long-Term Care: Challenges for the Aging Network in the 1990's.* Waltham, Mass.: National Aging Resource Center, Brandeis University.

Foster, B. H. et al., 1988. "Workforce Diversity and Business." *Training and Development Journal* (April): 38–42.

Pendleton, S. et al., 1990. "State Infrastructure for Long-Term Care: A National Study of State Systems, 1989." Waltham, Mass.: National Aging Resource Center, Brandeis University.

Peterson, D., Wendts, P. and Douglass, E., 1991. "Determining the Impact of Gerontology Preparation on Personnel in the Aging Network: A National Survey." Los Angeles: University of Southern California, Andrus Gerontology Center.

Watson, W. and Clayton, O., 1988. "Minority Manpower in the Field of Aging: Executive Summary." Atlanta, Ga: Center on Health and Aging.

Watson, W. and Clayton, O., 1989. "Education and Career Development of Minorities in Gerontology: The Significance of Gender, Curriculum Design, Race Relations and Population Growth." Atlanta, Ga.: Center on Health and Aging.

Scannel, A., 1989. "Targeting Outreach to Ethnic Minority Elderly: A Study of AAA Contracting Agencies and Aging Services Division Branch Offices in Multinomah County, Oregon." Portland, Oreg.: Institute on Aging, Portland State University.

Chapter 18

A Multicultural Conference: The Experience of New Mexico's Aging Network

Stephanie FallCreek and Rebecca Bustamante

New Mexico is one of the most ethnically and culturally diverse states in terms of the composition of its elder population. According to the 1990 census, 25.9 percent are Hispanic, 4.4 percent are American Indian, 1.3 percent are black, and 0.3 percent are Asian or Pacific Islander. This multicultural population has presented both challenges and opportunities to providers and advocates who develop and deliver education and training programs for the aging network.

The annual New Mexico Conference on Aging, now in its 13th year, provides a model for presenting a statewide conference that responds effectively to a very diverse population.

The annual conference, currently attracting about a thousand participants, offers a rich variety of opportunities for education, training, entertainment, and networking. Registrants include service providers, elected and appointed officials, aging network advocates, and consumers. The program, offered over a three-day period, is often preceded and followed by networking meetings, intensives, and special interest group workshops.

The success of the conference in responding to the ethnic and cultural diversity of the aging network lies primarily in the composition of the conference planning committee and its planning and implementation process. The committee has primary responsibility and authority for developing the program, setting fees, soliciting support, and recruiting participants. It works closely with the New Mexico State Agency on Aging (SAOA) staff, which also provides a significant portion of the administrative and clerical support needed to offer a conference of this magnitude.

The committee reflects the ethnic and cultural diversity of the aging network, always including both service provider and consumer representatives from at least the Anglo, Hispanic, and American Indian communities as well as both rural and urban areas. Aging network staff is represented, including the SAOA, area agencies on aging, and senior centers. For the 1991 conference, there were 22 organizational sponsors, each of whom was invited to name a representative to the committee. Although the exact composition of the committee varies from year to year, very diverse constituencies are always represented. In 1991, for example, these included the SAOA, the Northern New Mexico Economic Development District, the Hispanic Council on Aging, the New Mexico Indian Council on Aging, the Title VI Coalition, AARP, the Senior Coalition, ACTION programs, and the Commission on the Status of Women.

The diverse conference participants are attracted by the location, affordability, and responsive program of the conference. A centrally located, peaceful mountain-retreat conference center, with extremely reasonable prices (two nights and seven meals for $75.60 per person, with three to a room, plus a registration fee of $15 for those 60 and over and $25 for those under 60), has been the setting for the past 11 years.

Creating the program itself, however, is the most important aspect of responding to the diversity of needs and interests in New Mexico's aging network. The full committee determines the theme and keynote speakers for the conference, while the program subcommittee solicits and selects proposals for the presentations, assuring a balance of provider and consumer interest and beginner to advanced level of information.

Since the primary language of many elders is not English, several workshops are typically offered in Spanish or one of the American Indian dialects. These presentations are usually part of the consumer-oriented program track. Other workshops are offered in English, but the content is directed toward a specific ethnic community. For New Mexico's American Indian elders, whose tribes and pueblos share no common spoken or written language, sessions are often presented in English with native-speaking staff available to translate as needed. Presenters in these sessions are representatives of the target audiences.

An additional component that reflects and responds to New Mexico's ethnic diversity is the recognition award. Since 1984, each conference has recognized and honored individuals for their contributions to the aging network. Nominations for the award are solicited throughout the network, and the recipients are chosen by an appointed committee. Of the 53 awards bestowed to date, 14 have been given to Hispanics and 5 to American Indian elders.

In the 1991 program, some examples of the targeted sessions included Servicios para la Gente; SSI Indian Outreach Initiatives; Chicharones, Cracklins, and Achalon; and Hispanic Merchants Along the Santa Fe Trail. In previous years, sessions such as Growing Old with Health and Wisdom (Spanish, English, American Indian dialects); Remedios, Consejos y Tratamientos; Assessing Services for Rural Indian Elderly; Smoking Cessation for the Elder (English and Spanish); and a three-part session on the needs of rural minority elders have been offered.

Just as the session content responds to the ethnic diversity of the network, presenters also reflect this diversity. In the 1991 program, 28 of 72 sessions used one or more ethnic minority presenters. The fact that many session leaders are part of New Mexico's various ethnic communities enhances the credibility of the conference and increases the "comfort level" of elders who might not otherwise attend a conference-type event. Although exact figures are not available, reasonably accurate estimates indicate that participants at the 1990 conference included at least 7 percent American Indians and 37 percent Hispanics. Attendance of low-income elders and those attending for the first time, as well as elder program volunteers, is supported by local program fund-raisers and a variety of scholarships offered by aging network organizations. For example, the Hispanic Council on Aging offers a scholarship, and scholarship support by means of SAOA funds is also offered through the area agencies on aging, the Title VI programs, and the Navajo nation.

Although the annual conference has been highly effective in reaching and responding to New Mexico's ethnic diversity, the committee recognizes that work in this area will always be required. As the population continues to change, so do the needs and interests of the elders. The growing black and Asian elder populations need to be better represented, as do other distinct populations of elders like the developmentally disabled and the homeless. The crucial component is the recognition of diversity and the desire to respond to it.

The essential ingredients of a "New Mexico–style recipe" for responding to ethnic and cultural diversity are not mysterious or even very rare. They may not, however, always be easy to obtain. First, providers, consumers, and advocates who are capable of and committed to responding must be identified and cultivated. Second, a willingness to be flexible in planning and to respond to feedback must be present. Third, one or more persons in positions of authority and visibility must support and promote the idea that priority should be given to addressing the needs and interests of an ethnically diverse population. With these ingredients, a healthy and vital diversity of program and participants is highly likely.

Over time, given this approach, the historical experience of working together on conference planning and participating, within and across ethnic group membership lines, becomes a powerful force. The experience can assist the aging network to respond effectively to the diversity of its membership in accomplishing the larger mission of working collaboratively for the independence and dignity of all older persons.

Chapter 19

Dana Is Joy:
A Volunteer Caregivers' Program
in the Buddhist Tradition

Jeanette C. Takamura

In the Buddhist religion, the concept of *dana* or "selfless giving" is the first virtue among the Six *Paramitas* or Perfections. According to Hajime Nakamura, the foremost Buddhist scholar in Japan, *dana* is the ideal practice of the *Bodhisattva* or the "person who is seeking to attain buddhahood" or "whose mind (*sattva*) is fixed on *bodhi* (enlightment)" (Nakamura, 1987). It is giving that occurs with "an unattached and spontaneous mind" (Guenther, 1958), that is, it "is not done 'for the sake of others' but . . . 'for one's own joy' " (Makino, 1990). From the Buddhist perspective, *dana* is not giving that "is directed solely for the sake of others, . . . [for that would be] simply imitation and not true *dana*. Interestingly, the Chinese character 'imitation' is composed of two other parts which read 'for the sake of' and 'others' " (Makino, 1990).

Ultimately, dana is the "most profound among all joys . . . that which is found through witnessing and experiencing the joy of others [so that] . . . the joy of others becomes one's own joy. Making the joy of others your own joy manifests the true spirit of *dana* (Makino, 1990).

For the members of the Moiliili Hongwanji Mission in metropolitan Honolulu, Dana is joy. Project Dana, a nonsectarian caregivers' program, was first conceived in 1989 to address the needs of the frail and homebound through assistance by volunteers. The purpose of the project is simply to offer spiritual, emotional, and physical care to those who are homebound and frail.

Barely one year old, the project has offered more than 110 persons over 5,000 hours of services, including friendly home visits, caregivers' relief, hospital and nursing home visits, telephone reassurance, help with minor home repairs and housekeeping, and transportation to stores, church, and medical appointments. Volunteers of all ages and from all walks of life are drawn from within the Buddhist community, primarily from the Moiliili Hongwanji Mission. While the average age of those receiving help from Project Dana volunteers is 78.4 years, the youngest is 36 and the oldest 101.

All Dana volunteers are given six hours of training over nearly a three-month period. They are taught how to listen, how to provide a caring presence reflecting the Buddhist virtues, and how to serve those in need. They learn about community resources and the fundamentals pertaining to recordkeeping, assessment tools, insurance forms, and confidential documents. They are also provided with an introduction to the physical, social, and psychological aspects of aging.

Before volunteers are matched with clients, home assessments are made and volunteer profiles are examined. Considerations such as the client's needs, interests, and language preference are noted, as are the volunteer's interests, capabilities, and geographic availability. After a match is completed, the Project Dana administrator and her associates attempt to determine client and volunteer satisfaction with the arrangement and the caregiving expectations and outcomes.

Dana clients clearly are pleased with the assistance they are receiving. Just as pleased are the volunteers who are giving of themselves. As Kelly Kanetani reported:

> Since April [1990] I have been a companion to an 83-year-old woman. . . . My visits have evolved from that tentative and nervous first visit to visits filled with conversation and sharing. Some of the things we do together during these visits include sharing photographs and stories about our families, talking about activities we've both done since the last visit, watching TV, reading the Sunday paper, and eating lunch. To show her appreciation, my friend never lets me leave her house empty-handed. Fruits, chips, bread, and *manju* [sweet bean cake] are just some of the things she gives me before I leave. My friend has helped me to understand the true meaning of *dana*.

In metropolitan Honolulu, Dana is joy!

ACKNOWLEDGMENT

The author would like to acknowledge Shimeji Kanazawa, Rose Nakamura, Makoto Kunimune, the Reverend Shigenori Makino, and the Reverend Yoshiaki Fujitani for their assistance with this chapter.

REFERENCES

Guenther, H. V., 1958. *Jewel Ornament of Liberation.* Berkeley, Calif.: Shambala Publications, p. 153.

Kouzuki, N., 1990. "Project Dana." *The White Way* 34(5):5.

Makino, S., 1990. "Dana Is a Joy (II)." *The White Way* 34(2):3.

Nakamura, H., 1987. "Bodhisattva Path." In M. Eliade, ed., *Encyclopedia of Religions,* vol. 2. New York: Macmillan, p. 265.

Chapter 20

The Village of O'tabe: Tribal Officials and Service Providers Coordinate Comprehensive Support for Elders

Curtis D. Cook

With a reasonable amount of effort, one may find tucked away high in the Mogollon Rim country of Arizona the Indian village of O'tabe. This small Indian community is one of the few remaining places in America where people have not forgotten how to respect their elders. In fact, the elders of O'tabe are the central focus of community life. Virtually the entire village—neighbors, family members, tribal officials, service providers, even the young people—all work together to ensure a safe, healthy, and secure environment for their elders.

Not long ago, tribal officials and service providers met together to discuss and implement an Elder Focus campaign in which the entire service delivery infrastructure is coordinated through a central focal point, an Office of Senior Affairs (OSA), and is designed to support the elders in their homes, providing the services they need when they need them. Envisioned was a genuine continuum of care and services in the context of a sensitive and responsive community—a community where elders are still venerated and are seen as valuable and contributing members of the society.

Service providers and others who are to be involved in the service delivery system go through a period of orientation, in which they receive information on the local history, culture, social structures and values, for the purpose of sensitizing them to the needs of the elders. A serendipitous result of this sensitizing effort is that it fosters a spirit of cooperation and respect, in which service providers characteristically give more of themselves to the privilege of serving others. This brings about a synergism that adds to the effectiveness and comprehensiveness of services, which, in turn, help to assure that services to other age cohorts are not compromised as the elders receive priority. Duties become viewed as opportunities, adding significantly to the quality of life of all O'tabe residents.

Through negotiation between tribal leaders, advocates, representatives of the OSA, and state and federal officials, agreements are struck that help to remove jurisdictional and regulatory barriers to access. Similarly, cooperative agreements are also developed between service provider agencies, helping to eliminate "turfism" and gaps or overlap in the delivery of services. Here is a brief description of the O'tabe Elder Focus campaign:

OFFICE OF SENIOR AFFAIRS

The OSA is a central coordinating point for the array of services and programs in the village that address the needs of the elders. Maintaining complete files on each elder and working in conjunction with the senior center, the OSA assures proper coordination of core Older Americans Act services (congregate and home-delivered meals, transportation, and information and referral). Other supportive services are provided through other Elder Focus component programs. The OSA receives reports on the elders' needs and refers this information to other Elder Focus entities for appropriate response.

The OSA is supported by three sources: (1) Older Americans Act Title III and Title VI funds, (2) state-administered Title XX funds, and (3) an allocation from the tribal indirect-cost pool and other tribal funds.

ELDER ASSIST

The Elder Assist campaign is a communitywide effort in which community members give two to four hours per week providing various kinds of assistance to the elders. The registrants are young people, neighbors, relatives, tribal employees, skilled laborers, and so forth, who perform chore services, shopping assistance, cutting of fuel wood, minor household repairs, respite care, and similar services. Needs lists, compiled through reports received by the OSA, are maintained, and tasks are assigned as each Elder Assist volunteer checks in, on a weekly basis. Volunteers turn in Elder Assist task reports, in which they identify the services completed and other needs observed during their visits in the elders' homes. Materials and goods for the completion of tasks are provided through donations of local businesses, leftovers materials from federally supported construction projects, tribal funds, and contributions of community members through the Elder Aid campaign.

ELDER CARE

Elder Care is a health-oriented treatment and prevention effort. It involves the Indian Health Service (IHS), Community Health Representatives (CHRs), the tribal Home Health Agency, the Senior Companion Program, health promotion specialists from the State Health Department, and other trained personnel—all working in coordinated fashion to provide the essential care needed to maintain the elders in their homes. Most of the clients come to this program through referrals coordinated by the OSA. A multidisciplinary team, led by the IHS, performs a health status assessment on each elder in the OSA client files and develops a care and treatment protocol that includes social service needs as well as needs for healthcare. Overlap and jurisdictional questions between the agencies are minimized through careful observance of the existing cooperative agreements.

ELDER SAFE

The Bureau of Indian Affairs, the Department of Housing and Urban Development, the Indian Health Service, the tribal administration, and others cooperate to perform a complete safety audit periodically in the home of each elder. Needs identified through this process are referred to the appropriate Elder Focus component through the OSA in the form of a work order. Life-threatening conditions receive top priority response from the system.

ELDER WATCH

Elder Watch is a community-based monitoring effort providing special training to families, Elder Assist volunteers, public utility workers, and others in the recognition and reporting of signs of elder abuse and neglect or in the identification of hazardous conditions that may jeopardize the elders. As with other Elder Focus components, referrals to response entities are channeled through the OSA.

ELDER ALERT

Community volunteers, CHRs, and others receive first-responder training from Elder Alert in preparation for appropriate response to emergencies. In addition to a newly-installed 911 telephone notification system that links homes with the emergency medical services, fire department, and police, each elder is also given an individual emergency notification unit. An elder need only press a button on an electronic signaling device to call for emergency assistance.

ELDER SHELTER

In reported cases of abuse or neglect, Elder Shelter, an adult protective services (APS) program, provides protection and intervention on the basis of a prescribed APS code. This code contains an Elders' Bill of Rights, which has been adopted by the tribal officials, and is enforced with uncompromising care for the safety and well-being of the elders. There is also a facility in the village that provides temporary shelter for an elder who is discovered to be in an especially abusive or neglectful situation, one that places the elder in serious jeopardy.

ELDERS' RIGHTS

Elders' Rights is a legal assistance program in which the OSA makes referrals to state-provided legal aid or to the tribal courts, in cases where the elders' rights have been violated.

ELDER AID

A community fund-raising campaign promoted periodically by the OSA and cooperating Elder Focus components, service organizations, and churches, Elder Aid generates contributions and other special assistance to elders in urgent need.

Other Elder Focus campaigns are being considered by the tribe for implementation in the near future: *Elder Link* (a special effort to get elders enrolled in entitlement programs), *Elder House* (a specialized housing project funded by HUD), *Elder Share* (an intergenerational program that enhances communication between elders and young people), and *Elder Corps* (a senior employment and training program).

Does all this sound too good to be true? There is today no such Indian community as O'tabe—but there oughtta be! And with a reasonable amount of effort, there can be. Some Indian communities have implemented programs similar to components of an Elder Focus campaign. The Cheyenne River Sioux in South Dakota, for instance, provide elderly "manors," where elders live in small clustered settings with family members nearby and where in-home services are provided as needed. Zuni Pueblo in New Mexico has a special health promotion program that coordinates other community health programs through the senior center in such a way that it approximates the Elder Care concept. But nowhere in Indian country is a concept like the Elder Focus campaign being implemented in its entirety. It is time for service providers, policy makers, tribal leaders, and advocates to get together and start building better communities—with respect to their elders.

Contributors

SHARE DeCROIX BANE is director, Center on Aging Studies, National Resource Center for Rural Elderly, University of Missouri, Kansas City.

VERN L. BENGTSON, Ph.D., is professor, Division of Social and Behavioral Science, University of Southern California, Los Angeles.

CHERYL J. BURNS, M.S.W., is a doctoral student in the Joint Program in Social Work and Sociology, University of Michigan, Ann Arbor.

LINDA M. BURTON, Ph.D., is associate professor, Department of Human Development and Family Studies, Pennsylvania State University, University Park.

REBECCA BUSTAMANTE is a manager, New Mexico State Agency on Aging, Sante Fe.

JOHN A. CAPITMAN, Ph.D., is research professor at the National Aging Resource Center: Long-Term Care, Brandeis University, Waltham, Massachusetts.

CURTIS D. COOK is a gerontologist who resides in Albuquerque, New Mexico.

NEAL E. CUTLER, Ph.D., is president and scientific director, Boettner Institute of Financial Gerontology, Bryn Mawr, Pennsylvania.

PEGGYE DILWORTH-ANDERSON, Ph.D., is professor, Department of Human Development and Family Studies, University of North Carolina, Greensboro.

STEPHANIE FALLCREEK is principal, FallCreek and Associates, Santa Fe, New Mexico.

DONALD GELFAND, Ph.D., is professor, School of Social Work, University of Maryland at Baltimore.

ROSE C. GIBSON, Ph.D., is faculty associate, Institute for Social Research, and associate professor, School of Social Work, University of Michigan, Ann Arbor.

DAVID E. HAYES-BAUTISTA, Ph.D., is professor of medicine and director, Chicano Studies Research Center, University of California, Los Angeles.

WINNIE HERNANDEZ-GALLEGOS, M.P.H., is research associate at the National Aging Resource Center: Long-Term Care, Brandeis University, Waltham, Massachusetts.

LOUISE M. KAMIKAWA is director of marketing, American Red Cross, Washington, D.C.

NEAL KRAUSE, Ph.D., is associate professor, School of Public Health, and associate research scientist, Institute of Gerontology, University of Michigan, Ann Arbor.

CARMELA G. LACAYO is president and CEO, Asociación Nacional Pro Personas Mayores and El Pueblo Community Development Corporation, Los Angeles, California.

SHIRLEY A. LOCKERY, Ph.D., is assistant professor, School of Social Work, Ann Arbor, Michigan.

MEREDITH MINKLER, Dr. P.H., is professor and chair, Health Education Program, School of Public Health, University of California, Berkeley.

EDGAR E. RIVAS is director, National Eldercare Institute on Transportation (Community Transportation Association of America), Washington, D.C.

JOAN ROBERTS is assistant coordinator, National Resource Center on Minority Aging Populations, University Center on Aging, San Diego State University, San Diego, California.

JOHN H. SKINNER, Ed.D., is associate dean and associate professor, College of Public Health, University of South Florida, Tampa.

E. PERCIL STANFORD, Ph.D., is professor and director, University Center on Aging, San Diego State University, San Diego, California.

JEANETTE C. TAKAMURA, Ph.D., is director of the Executive Office on Aging, Office of the Governor, State of Hawaii, Honolulu.

FERNANDO M. TORRES-GIL, Ph.D., is professor of social welfare, University of California, Los Angeles.

WILBUR H. WATSON, Ph.D., is professor of sociology, Morehouse College, Atlanta, Georgia.

LINDA A. WRAY is a doctoral candidate, Andrus Gerontology Center, University of Southern California, Los Angeles.

BARBARA W. K. YEE, Ph.D., is assistant professor of clinical gerontology, Graduate Studies Department, School of Allied Health Sciences, University of Texas Medical Branch, Galveston.

DONNA L. YEE, Ph.D., is senior research associate, Florence Heller School, Bigel Institute, Brandeis University, Waltham, Massachusetts.